Eleanor Roosevelt, with Love

A CENTENARY REMEMBRANCE

Eleanor Roosevelt, with Love

A CENTENARY REMEMBRANCE

ELLIOTT ROOSEVELT

Illustrated with photographs

LODESTAR BOOKS   E. P. DUTTON   NEW YORK

LIBRARY OF CONGRESS CATALOGING IN PUBLICATION DATA

Roosevelt, Elliott, date
  Eleanor Roosevelt, with love.

  "Lodestar books."
  Bibliography: p.
  Includes index.
    1. Roosevelt, Eleanor, 1884-1962. 2. Presidents—United States—Wives—Biography. 3. Roosevelt, Franklin D. (Franklin Delano), 1882-1945. I. Title.
E807.1.R48R655 1984 973.917'092'4 [B] 84-8013
ISBN 0-525-67147-1

Published in the United States by E. P. Dutton, Inc.
2 Park Avenue, New York, N.Y. 10016

Published simultaneously in Canada by
Fitzhenry & Whiteside Limited, Toronto

Editor: Virginia Buckley   Designer: Riki Levinson

Printed in the U.S.A.   COBE   First Edition
10 9 8 7 6 5 4 3 2 1

Frontispiece photograph credit: © HALSMAN, N.Y.

to my beloved Patricia,
who has shared with me
so much joy and sorrow
over the years

CONTENTS

Eleanor Roosevelt, with Love

A CENTENARY REMEMBRANCE

Eleanor Roosevelt, with Love

The later, or mature, years of Eleanor Roosevelt's life were marked by my father's election to the presidency of the United States, and ended with her death in New York, in 1962. In this period, Mother grew in stature not only as first lady but as the true partner of her husband. It is during this time that she found out that it really was possible to better the lot of many who needed assistance.

During her years in the White House, she set for herself a breakneck schedule of travel to every corner of our country. Individuals knew that if they addressed a letter to her their pleas for assistance would not go unnoticed. A letter to my mother always brought an immediate investigation by a proper government agency and if the request set forth had merit, it was dealt with speedily. She saw to it that the usual red tape and snail's pace of government agencies were eliminated and that immediate action could be counted on. It was through her efforts that the United States government gained a reputation, never achieved before or since, for fast action.

Throughout the Depression, she visited people from all

walks of life who had been devastated by the faltering economy. Later, she showed her concern for the welfare of all of those who were serving in the military, or on the homefront, in producing the materiel necessary for our war effort. Women were playing an increasing role in this all-out effort, and Mother took particular pains to see to it that their endeavors were properly appreciated and compensated.

With the death of my father and her appointment by President Harry S. Truman to the United Nations, Mother's activities became worldwide in scope. From 1945 on, she exerted her influence on a global stage. Her travels to every section of the world became as commonplace as her national travels had been in the years before. It was her example that encouraged the emergence of many feminine leaders in nations around the world. She counted among her close friends such future leaders of their countries as Indira Gandhi, the daughter of India's Prime Minister Nehru, and another woman destined to become the leader of her country, Golda Meir of Israel. In the emerging nations of the Third World, women had been traditionally regarded as incapable of occupying high offices of state. But, with the elevation of Eleanor Roosevelt to international prominence, many of these countries recognized the capabilities of women in their own countries and brought them into high positions of trust and responsibility.

My mother's philosophy was that war was a scourge to be eliminated from the earth. She felt that women throughout the world were devoted to the cause of the elimination of violence more wholeheartedly than men. As a result, she worked indefatigably to arouse the women of the world to take more responsibility in the direction of establishing the policies of their governments.

If she were alive today, she would have worked for the passage of the Equal Rights Amendment to the Constitution. Her argument would have been that women had a right and duty to work side by side with men in all phases of life. She would have abhorred the necessity of a military draft, but if such a draft was required to insure the national safety of our country, she would have felt that women should be drafted alongside the men, and that they should be given the responsibility of assignment to combat, in the same fashion as men. She did not believe that there was any job, in any phase of life, that a woman could not do as well as, or better than, any man.

In her experience, once she had made up her mind to overcome any odds that were against her; she did so with unrelenting determination and single-minded effort. For here was a woman whose very background and early training had left her totally unprepared for the host of challenges that she was called upon to face during her lifetime. She not only reeducated herself to meet these challenges, but she accepted the responsibility of conquering them. When my mother died, her body was physically worn out, but she died content knowing that she had never turned away from facing any crisis and that, in the end, she had conquered all.

As a son, I am profoundly conscious of the fact that Mother exerted an enormous influence on the world in which we live today. In all my contacts with her throughout her life, I came to realize that her love for her fellow human beings was not confined to her loved ones, friends, or even acquaintances. She was constantly reaching out a hand of friendship and compassion to all people who came in contact with her. Her tireless travels around the world brought her in touch with hundreds of millions of people. Through her work in the United Nations, she established relationships with people in every corner of the world.

I realize that today there are probably billions of people who weren't even alive when Mother died. These people cannot possibly comprehend the immense impact that her efforts have had on the daily lives of all of us today. The great surge of the human rights movement of the seventies, which started with so much promise in 1972 with the Helsinki Accords and was followed with the well-meaning Carter Administration's drive for human rights recognition on a global scale, was evidence of her direct influence. Her devotion to the elimination of racial and religious discrimination became an integral part of the philosophy of many nations. Her tireless efforts have helped bring about the realization that war solves no problems, that war is totally destructive, and that a state of preparedness for war undermines the economic well-being of all nations.

In various parts of the world today, there are hundreds of thousands of people demanding a nuclear freeze. These hundreds of thousands are echoing her beliefs. The struggles of the blacks in our country, the struggles of the emerging nations—with largely black or other colored populations—were first championed by my mother. It was her firm belief that equal educational opportunities should be provided for all, everywhere, in every nation. She believed that this was the only way to bring about an understanding of the necessity for peaceful coexistence. She also believed that health was a primary consideration and, above all, she was firmly dedicated to the premise that malnutrition and starvation could prevent peace in the world as surely as a nuclear bomb.

As her descendants, you and I can take hope from her example that a way can be found to solve the problems that seem so insoluble to many of us today.

1

The Early Years

Anna Hall, in the words of my mother, belonged to a segment of New York City society that thought itself all-important. According to my mother, in that society you were kind to the poor, you did not neglect your philanthropic duties, you assisted the hospitals, and you did something for the needy. You accepted invitations to dine and to dance only with the right people, and you lived in their midst. You thought seriously about your children's education, and you read the books that everybody read, and you were familiar with good literature. In short, you conformed to the conventional pattern. Anna Hall, who was my mother's mother, was extremely beautiful and was much in demand in her social circle.

At nineteen, Anna Hall married Elliott Roosevelt. He was charming, good-looking, loved by all who came in contact with him, but he had a background and upbringing that were alien to Anna Hall's pattern. My mother said that he had a weakness which he probably never quite understood. If he had lived in today's world, his illness would have been quickly diagnosed, but in those days, medicine had no way of detecting hidden growths. Elliott Roosevelt, when he was fifteen and at St. Paul's School in New Hampshire, was smitten with excruciatingly painful and blinding headaches. Sometimes these attacks were so severe that he fainted away. These attacks were to continue throughout the next sixteen years. During those years, the pain and pressure within his head became so unbearable that he turned to alcohol as a relief.

The marriage of Anna and Elliott took place in 1881. This was to be a tragically short marriage with very few moments of happiness. During their marriage, Anna and Elliott spent precious little time together because of his erratic behavior. There were three children born to the marriage. Mother was born on October 11, 1884; she had two younger brothers, Elliott, Jr., and Hall, but Mother's world was thrown into confusion when she was barely eight years old. On December 7, 1892, her mother and her little brother Ellie both died from diphtheria. In those days, there was no way that the medical profession could counter this grim disease. Tragedy was again to overwhelm her on August 14, 1894, just before she became ten years of age. Her father died, and only then was it discovered that for many years he had had an active and growing tumor of the brain, which had finally brought him to his early death. Mother was an orphan from this day forward.

She had a legal guardian who was to look after her affairs. This person was Theodore Roosevelt, her father's brother, who was later to become president of the United States. He was already extremely taken up with his political career, so Mother's life was directed by her maternal grandmother, Anna Hall, for whom Eleanor's mother had been named. Actually, her grandmother was not at all impressed with the Roosevelts of Oyster Bay, and she saw to it that Eleanor Roosevelt spent as little time as possible with her Uncle Ted, or any of the other relatives on her father's side of the family.

During Mother's childhood years, her beautiful mother had

Eleanor with her doting father, 1889   FRANKLIN D. ROOSEVELT LIBRARY

Eleanor with her father and brother Hall   FRANKLIN D. ROOSEVELT
LIBRARY

often shown her displeasure over the fact that her daughter was an "ugly duckling." Her mother made a great effort, reading to her daughter or having her daughter read to her. She would have Mother recite poems, and keep her up after the brothers had gone to bed. In spite of the attention, Mother recalled standing in the door, often with her finger in her mouth, and she could see the disdainful look in her mother's eyes and hear the mocking tone of her voice as she said, "Come in, Granny." Mother wanted to sink through the floor in shame. Mother's maternal aunt, Elizabeth Hall, who was known as Tissie, was as beautiful as her mother. She too would often make disparaging remarks about the ungainly and awkward little girl. Even her mother's brothers were not above teasing little Eleanor. Therefore, it is not at all strange that Eleanor Roosevelt grew up in those very early years with a sense of timidity, and as her adolescent years approached, she became more and more introspective and hesitant in the company of others.

Her Roosevelt relatives were a friendly and outgoing group of people. Their company could greatly have reduced the introverted outlook of the little girl. But this was not to be, because Grandmother Hall severely limited her contacts with that side of the family. Even while her mother was alive, little Eleanor had been sent off to a convent in France, to get her out of the way when her baby brother Hall was about to arrive. She was not even six years old at the time, and she found the experience away from home to be a very unhappy one. Finally, in 1899, when she was fifteen, she was sent off to England to attend the Allenswood School, which was close to London, and not far from Wimbledon Common. This school was run by a very remarkable lady, Mlle. Marie Souvestre. She became enormously fond of Mlle. Souvestre, and the time that she spent in that school greatly aided her in acquiring a fine, basic education that was to stand her in good stead throughout her life. She became fluent in French and could converse tolerably well in German and Italian. She returned home after three years to take her place in New York society.

She had a very maternal attitude toward her younger brother, Hall, and when he entered Groton in the fall of 1903, it was she who accompanied him to the boarding school in Massachusetts. She lived with her aunt, Mrs. Mortimer, and found that she was automatically on the social list to "come out" that season. Little did my mother realize what an agony it would be to have to attend all the debutante balls. Here was a girl who had never learned to dance very well and who had none of the social graces that would enable her to carry on animated small talk with all the young men whom she was about to meet. It was very difficult for a young girl who knew practically none of the young men who attended these parties. In those days, when you went to a dance, you were given a card on which the young men were supposed to enter their names for the particular dances that they wished to have with a young lady. In Mother's case, she had to go to every dance, knowing that there were precious few acquaintances who would rush over and enter their names on her card. It was all rather a nightmare.

There was one redeeming feature to this period of social activity. She became friends with her distant cousin, Franklin Roosevelt, and Franklin's cousin, Lyman Delano. These two young men were attending Harvard, and they introduced her to many of their college friends. Gradually, this new circle of college boys started to fill up her card, to the point where the dances could become pleasurable, rather than a towering bore.

Mother and Father had met many years before, when she was only two years old. Her parents had taken her to visit Mr. and Mrs. James Roosevelt, at Hyde Park, and while she was there, the five-year-old Franklin had played "horse" for little Eleanor in the nursery. Father's interest in Mother seems to have been almost instantaneous when they became reacquainted. He found her to be a fascinating conversationalist whom he wanted to know better. He would come down from

Harvard on weekends to visit Mother, and his interest became more and more ardent as the months went by. I think that a lovely part of the courtship of my parents was expressed by Mother way back in 1937 when she wrote, "It was understood that no girl was interested in a man or showed any liking for him until he made all the advances. You knew a man very well before you wrote or received a letter from him, and those letters make me smile when I see some of the correspondence today. There were few men who would have dared to use my first name, and to have signed oneself in any other way than 'very sincerely yours' would have been not only a breach of good manners but an admission of feeling which was entirely inadmissible. You never allowed a man to give you a present, except flowers or candy or possibly a book. To receive a piece of jewelry from a man to whom you were not engaged was a sign of being a fast woman, and the idea that you would permit any man to kiss you before you were engaged to him never even crossed my mind. I had painfully high ideals and a tremendous sense of duty entirely unrelieved by any sense of humor or any appreciation of the weaknesses of human nature. Things were either right or wrong for me, and I had too little experience to know how fallible human judgments are."

She had great curiosity about life and a desire to participate in every experience that might be the lot of a woman. She felt the urge to hurry and be a part of the mainstream and so in the autumn of 1903, when Franklin Roosevelt, her fifth cousin once removed, asked her to marry him, it seemed entirely natural. She never even gave a thought to the fact that they were both very young and very inexperienced. As a mature women, she was to comment, "Yet I know now that it was years later before I understood what being in love or what loving really meant."

How painfully innocent and unprepared this mother of mine must have been for the marriage which was to take place on March 17, 1905.

Father's mother, Sarah Delano Roosevelt, was not very

My mother poses in her wedding dress.   PACH BROS. / BETTMANN
ARCHIVE, INC.

happy when she learned of Franklin's intention to marry Eleanor. She tried her best to take his mind off what she considered a temporary infatuation, and that winter she sent him away from his studies for a winter cruise to the West Indies, hoping that his ardor would cool. In the meantime, a very miserable Eleanor was left alone in New York. But, evidently, Franklin's feelings did not change.

It is interesting to note in recalling the history of Franklin and Eleanor Roosevelt's life that their marriage date was set by the necessity of the president of the United States to be in New York on that particular day. The date of the marriage was set for St. Patrick's Day, March 17, 1905, because President Theodore Roosevelt was coming to New York for the parade on that day. He was to give the bride in marriage, so it was arranged that he would do so following the parade.

They were married in the house of Mother's cousin, Susie Parish, and the reception was held after the ceremony. Of course, the presence of the president of the United States heightened the sense of excitement for the guests at the wedding. The bride and groom were to receive the guests in the front sitting room of the house, and the president and other members of the family were to form a receiving line. Teddy Roosevelt, feeling that he was taking away attention from the bride and groom, left the receiving line and went back to the back parlor on the same floor. As if on signal, all the guests and the remaining members of the family removed themselves from the front sitting room and left the bride and groom standing alone at their own wedding reception. Maybe this is when it first came into my father's mind that he would have to, himself, become president of the United States, if he wanted to have any attention.

❧ 2 ❧

Out of the Cocoon

After the wedding, Father and Mother went on a honeymoon to Europe. Both of them had been to Europe before, and so both had very favorite places to visit. But this trip was particularly exciting for them. They really felt like adults and not just young people. They learned a great deal about each other's likes and dislikes. On their return, they found that Sarah Delano Roosevelt, father's mother, had already taken charge of their lives. She had picked out a house for them in New York City. She furnished each room, mostly with selections from her other residences. She had a summer cottage at Campobello Island in New Brunswick, Canada, and early in their marriage she bought the cottage next door to hers for the young couple.

Mother settled in to her new existence without too much turmoil. The truth of the matter was that she knew nothing about housekeeping. She couldn't cook, and the mysteries of the laundry were completely beyond her. Of course, this admitted innocent of all innocents got pregnant almost immediately, and a girl was born on May 3, 1906. It is lucky that Father's mother was fairly well-to-do, because Mother had to have lots of help in the house. She also knew nothing about

Newlyweds Franklin and Eleanor in Newburgh, New York, May
1905   FRANKLIN D. ROOSEVELT LIBRARY

taking care of a newborn babe, and so, for my sister, Anna
Eleanor, she had to have a nurse in to look after the child.

In the summer of 1906, the routine pattern of their life was
set. In the spring, the young family would go to visit at Hyde
Park for a time and then later in the summer they would journey up to Campobello. The summer would be spent at Campobello, until Labor Day, and then the return trip would be
made to Hyde Park. After a few weeks of enjoying the glorious
autumn on the Hudson River, the family would go back to New
York for the winter.

My grandmother, Sarah Delano Roosevelt, and Mother, sailing on their boat, the *Half Moon,* off Campobello Island, Canada   LAURA DELANO / FRANKLIN D. ROOSEVELT LIBRARY

During the fall and winter months, Father was preoccupied with finishing law school at Columbia University, and Mother was again busy producing offspring. On December 23, 1907, their first boy, James, was born. By this time, her mother-in-law felt that the house she had equipped for them was no longer adequate. With a rapidly growing family, what they needed was a house big enough to accommodate at least five or six children. My grandmother had two houses built on East Sixty-fifth Street in New York City, numbers 47 and 49 respectively. Both houses were extremely narrow. She made a point of hav-

[*18*]

ing connecting doors on almost every floor. She chose Number 47 for her own residence, and installed Father and Mother in Number 49. The following incident indicates how traumatic it was for my mother to live in such close proximity to her mother-in-law. A few weeks after they moved into the new house on East Sixty-fifth Street, Mother sat in front of her dressing table and wept, and when her bewildered husband asked her what on earth was the matter with her, she said that she did not like to live in a house which was not in any way hers. There was not one thing that she had done that represented the way she wanted to live. Father was perplexed; he thought she was quite mad and told her so gently. She allowed as how she would feel differently in a little while, and he left her alone until she regained her composure.

Over a ten-year period, Mother was always just getting over having a baby or about to have one. She was never very athletic, and so her physical exercise was confined to walking. On March 18, 1909, the first baby Franklin was born. That fall, all of the children came down with the flu, and little Franklin died on November 1, not quite eight months later. She immediately became pregnant again, and I came into the world on September 23, 1910.

By this time Father had graduated from law school and had been admitted to the bar. He was working in the firm of Carter, Ledyard, and Milburn. The urge to get into politics was so great that Father quickly abandoned his new law career to run for the state senate from his Hudson River district. Mother knew nothing about politics, and she hardly made any contribution to his campaign. In fact, she was very much astonished when election day rolled around and the returns showed that her Democratic-candidate husband had been elected. That district had not elected a Democrat in thirty-two years. Mother started the first of her many moves necessitated by the political career of her husband.

They rented their house in New York and moved to Albany.

Mother remarked that this move to Albany marked for the first time a dual existence for her, which was to last the rest of her life. She felt that it was her duty to be interested in whatever her husband was, whether "politics, books, or a particular dish for dinner." Mother's early training had always been that duty was perhaps the motivating force in one's life, often to the exclusion of any joy or pleasure. So she went about her duties of running a household and did her level best to understand the intricacies of political life. By June of 1912, she was sufficiently involved to attend a political convention, but Father was so busy that she soon lost interest. That was the year Woodrow Wilson was nominated on the Democratic ticket for president of the United States.

That summer Mother had gone back home and taken us children to Campobello. I was two years old. I had a nanny who was supposed to look after me because my parents believed I was knock-kneed, and the family doctor had encased both legs in hip-high braces. The result was a highly hyper youngster who maneuvered stiff-legged along the rocky beach below our house at Campobello.

On one particular day, Mother shooed Nanny and little Elliott out to join other youngsters in gathering driftwood on the beach and piling it up in a giant pile for a bonfire. Nanny let her attention wander from worrying about my movements. I stumbled as I approached the roaring and crackling fire and fell face forward into the flames and hot coals. My screams brought Nanny and many others to the rescue. I was dragged from the fire. Hot coals were still lodged between the leg braces and my skin. The hair on my head and my eyebrows had been burned off. I was still screaming from the pain of the burns ten minutes later, when Mother hove breathlessly into view.

She arranged for two grown-ups to carry me, with my legs still encased in the braces, up to the house. There, at last, they removed the braces, and bathed my body, from head to foot in burn cream.

Summers at Campobello were part of the family routine. I am three years old here with Mother.   FRANKLIN D. ROOSEVELT LIBRARY

Mother sent a messenger for the doctor to come over from Lubec, Maine. Hours later, he appeared. He declared the worst burns had been caused by red hot coals that lodged between the steel braces and my legs.

As I recovered, I begged Mother, time and again, never to make me wear those dreadful braces again. Mother resisted my entreaties for some time, but, finally, she gave in. I hugged and kissed her with great ferocity and swore she wouldn't be sorry. I have walked with a rolling, bowlegged gait from that day to this. Mother's decision turned my mind in the direction of wanting to be an honest-to-goodness cowboy when I grew up.

The following April, President Wilson sent for my father

and offered him the post of assistant secretary of the navy. Mother's favorite aunt, on her father's side of the family, Admiral William S. Cowles' wife, affectionately known as Auntie Bye, had a house at 1733 N Street, in Washington, D.C. She generously made this house available to her niece and nephew-in-law.

The autumn of 1913 marked the entrance of Mother into the highly sophisticated social and political life of our nation's capital. With the exception of a few years, from 1921 until 1932, she was to be deeply involved in the Washington scene for the rest of her life. There are some interesting sidelights in the evolution of her thinking that emerged at about this time. Throughout most of her early years, she had never had much contact with blacks. When she went to Washington, she found that most of the servants employed in the Washington area were black. In addition, Mother had had little contact with other minorities, particularly Jews. It was during her first years in Washington that Mother's real education began. She met all kinds of new people. For the first time, she realized that enormous frictions existed among religions, races, and even sections of the country.

Even a much more strenuous and demanding life as the wife of a subcabinet officer did not prevent her from getting pregnant again, and on August 17, 1914, the second baby Franklin was born at Campobello. That same summer, a terrible war broke out in Europe. This was the beginning of World War I.

By 1916, Mother had her last child. In March of that year, her fourth living son, John Aspinwall, was born. And it became more and more evident, in her contact with all the members of the government around her in Washington, that we Americans were going to be forced into the war. War was declared on April 6, 1917. Mother helped to organize the Navy Red Cross, and she immersed herself in war work. During this period of intense activity, Mother came across many very important na-

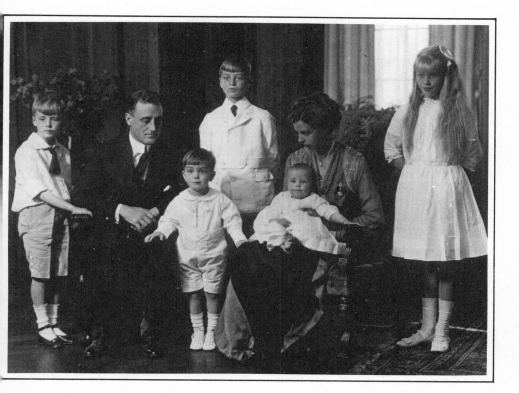

A family photo taken in Washington, D.C., in 1916. *Left to right:* Elliott, Father, Franklin, Jr., James, Mother, John (*on Mother's lap*), and Anna   HAROLD L. RITCH / FRANKLIN D. ROOSEVELT LIBRARY

tional and international figures who were contributing to the war effort. One of the most notable memories that Mother carried with her into later years was her account of a trip she made on the presidential yacht *Sylph* down to Mt. Vernon, on the Potomac River. On this trip Arthur Balfour of England, Marshal Joseph Joffre of France, and Premier René Viviani of Italy were the guests of honor. They laid a wreath on the tomb of George Washington. Mother recalled that when someone on the lawn at Mt. Vernon told Mr. Balfour the story of George Washington's throwing a silver dollar across the Potomac to the other shore, his eyes twinkled and he responded, "My dear sir, he accomplished an even greater feat than that. He threw a sovereign across the ocean!"

Immediately after the declaration of war, her Uncle Ted came down to Washington to offer his services to the president to raise a division to take to Europe. He felt that he would have no difficulties in enlisting the best officers in the army to serve under him, and that many of the old Rough Riders and the finest of the young men of America would want to go with him. He enlisted Mother's and Father's aid to intervene on his behalf with the president. No one could change President Wilson's attitude. He turned down Uncle Ted's request, and I am convinced that the disappointment of not being able to participate in the war was so great that Uncle Ted finally died in 1919 from a broken heart.

Father and Mother were apart a good deal of the time in 1917 and 1918. Father made a trip to Europe to inspect naval and marine units. When he returned, he came back with pneumonia. When he was taken off the ship, Mother unpacked his luggage. This was the time when Mother experienced the first really traumatic event of her married life. In the luggage she discovered a number of letters that he had received, which she opened and read. In her life, she had really had only two men who were all-important to her. The first, when she was a very little girl, had been her father. He showered love and affection on her, and she knew that she was the most important person in his life. A few years after he died, along came Franklin Delano Roosevelt. He became the center of her universe. She lived his life just as he wanted to live it. When she read those letters, she realized that during the long months when she was not beside him in Washington, he had formed a friendship with another woman. Frankly, she was shattered, and a stormy crisis developed. This woman had been her personal social secretary, Lucy Mercer. Finally, the crisis was resolved, and Mother and Father worked out an agreement. They decided to both go forward together and to make their marriage work. This was probably a very fortunate decision for Father, in light of the fact that only a few years later he was to be stricken with polio. It was Mother's determination to nurse him back into active life that really enabled him to overcome the effects of paralysis.

They both returned to the strenuous duties in Washington, and finally, on November 11, 1918, the Armistice was signed and the end of World War I came to pass. After the Armistice, they went to France and it was there they received the news by radio, on January 6, that her Uncle Ted had passed away.

At about this time, in the fall of 1919, Mother came in contact, for the first time, with an organization called the International Congress of Working Women. There were representatives from nineteen nations who met in Washington. This was Mother's first contact with an organization that was concerned with working conditions of women. Mother's interest was immediately attracted to this cause, and she set out to learn as much as possible about how women were treated in various parts of the world and particularly in our country. But her husband's career prevented her from becoming very active at this time, because in June of 1920, Father was nominated at the Democratic National Convention, in San Francisco, for vice president of the United States. His running mate on the ticket as the presidential nominee was James M. Cox of Ohio. They campaigned strenuously together, crisscrossing the country in trains. Mother was not very comfortable, as she was still not able to stand up in front of a gathering and give a talk. So her participation was confined to following Father around and listening to virtually the same speech being made at every whistle-stop.

The election itself was an overwhelming defeat. Harding and Coolidge were elected. By March 1921, Mother and Father had returned to New York, he to resume the practice of law, and she to become active in the League of Women Voters. Mother was to make her first tentative steps toward developing an independent life that would supplement her continued support of Father's career.

3

Father's Illness

I think that by 1921 Mother had been through some extremely serious crises, all of which had resulted in her becoming a much more mature and less naive individual. She no longer was dominated unquestioningly by her mother-in-law. She no longer was completely dependent upon a household staff to carry out the domestic affairs. When the family moved back to New York from Washington, after the presidential election of 1920, her own autobiography is quite revealing about this particular time.

She explained that her mother-in-law was distressed because she was not always available, as she had been when she lived in New York before. She had long since ceased to be dependent on her mother-in-law, and the fact that Mother's cousin, Mrs. Parish, suffered from a long illness, lasting several years, had made Mother less dependent on her also. She wrote fewer letters, asked fewer questions, and gave fewer confidences, for she had begun to realize that in her development she was drifting far afield from the old influences. That did not mean that she felt better for this, but she was thinking things out for herself and becoming more of an individual.

The winter of 1921 found Mother reaching out in a number of directions. She was working hard at expanding her contacts with others. She agreed to serve on the boards of directors of several charities and threw herself into the work of the League of Women Voters.

As usual, the summer of 1921 found the entire family moving back up to our place at Campobello. Father came up to join us in August after everyone was settled. He arrived on the yacht of Mr. Van Lear Black, who was the chairman of the board of the Maryland Casualty Company. Mr. Black was Father's employer, inasmuch as he had appointed Father general counsel of his insurance company earlier in the year.

One day after Mr. Black and his yacht had departed, Father decided, after a strenuous afternoon, that he would like to go for a swim on the other side of the island. There was a lake over there that all of us liked to use as a swimming hole, because it was much warmer than the Bay of Fundy. All five children accompanied him, and we had a glorious time swimming in the warm water. Then he led us all down across the beach for a quick dip in the ice cold waters of the bay. These waters very rarely got up to 48° F. in the summertime. After our swim, he challenged us kids to a race back to the house. Needless to say, the two youngest, Franklin and John, quickly fell behind, and Father slowed down to stay with them, during the last mile or so, back to the house. A good deal of mail had arrived during our absence, and Father sank back into a chair to look through the pile of letters.

After about an hour or so, he looked up at Mother and said that he felt chilled. He thought he would not join us for supper, but that he would go right up to bed and get under the warm blankets. He complained of aches in his back as he went up the stairs. The next morning he woke up with quite a fever. The nearest doctor was at Lubec, Maine, across the narrows from the island. Dr. Bennett had been our summer doctor for many years. He, at first, thought that Father's ailment was just an ordinary cold, but within three days he became thoroughly alarmed. Father's body from the neck down was becoming so sensitive that even the weight of a light blanket caused him tremendous pain. He was anxious to have a consultant physician.

A Dr. Keen was located at Bar Harbor, Maine, and he came up to consult with Dr. Bennett. By this time, the inflammation in the upper part of the body had subsided, but the lower part of his body was paralyzed. As the days dragged by, the doctors urged Mother to get skilled nurses on a twenty-four-hour basis. None were to be found, so Mother took total charge of nursing her stricken husband. Finally, a well-known infantile paralysis specialist, Dr. Robert Lovett, was brought up from Newport, Rhode Island. After he had examined Father, he took Mother aside and told her that Father had polio. All this time my grandmother, "Granny" to us, had been in Europe, but she arrived back soon after the diagnosis. It was decided that as soon as arrangements could be made, Father should be moved from the island back to a hospital in New York.

This move was accomplished with great difficulty. First of all, he had to be carried on an improvised stretcher from the house, down the hill, across a stony beach, to a small motorboat which carried him across the bay to Eastport, Maine, where he was lifted from the boat to the dock and finally was put through a window of the railroad car which was to carry him to New York City. Upon arrival in New York, he was rushed by ambulance to the Presbyterian Hospital on Park Avenue. There he was placed under the direct care of Dr. George Draper. Father stayed in the hospital for several months and finally came home just before Christmas.

Granny had made up her mind that Father would be an invalid for the rest of his life, and she determined that he would have to retire from active life and that he should go to Hyde Park to live there as a country squire.

All during these months of anxiety, Mother did much of the

nursing of Father, although she did get help. She remained constantly available and at his side to perform the duties that would make his recovery possible. Although he was in bed most of the time, and he was a tall and well-built man, she and the nurse managed to do all that was necessary. While she was devoting every effort to looking after Father, she was also carrying on all the domestic duties, running the household, looking after five children, and keeping up contacts with Father's law partners and her own outside activities.

Early on, she realized that a deep depression was affecting Father's mental outlook. She realized that the illness had raised doubts in his mind as to whether he could ever be active again. Father's mother was convinced of the same. Mother became alarmed at this attitude and she started out on a plan to arouse him from his lethargy. She enlisted the aid and support of Louis Howe, Father's longtime assistant and confidant. To accomplish this end, Louis Howe felt that Father's interest could best be aroused by keeping him in touch with the political scene. Louis Howe told Mother that she should get herself involved politically, not just as a passive supporter of her husband's career, but become personally active herself.

Mother proceeded to join the Women's Trade Union League, where she came in contact with many of the women that she had first met in Washington at the International Congress of Working Women. She then became a working member of an organization known as The Democratic Women of New York State, ending up as finance chairman of the Democratic State Committee. During this time, she worked at many humdrum political activities, such as driving a car on election day and taking people to the polls. She worked with the County Democratic Committee and learned a great deal about party politics, some of which she felt was rather sordid. On the other hand, she found that there were many people who worked hard and delivered unselfish public service. Gradually, her own interest in public service became much keener. She found that she was establishing a whole new group of friends and acquaintances. Her old friends from her previous life in New York became less and less involved in her new life. They were leading mostly social lives. She had dropped out of what is known as "society" entirely, and she was never to go back to it again.

Her new group of friends were all involved in the political scene in one way or another, either at the county, state, or national level, or they were women who were devoted to the promotion of women's place in the world. Father's interest was piqued by all the new activities that Mother was entering into in the political world, but it did not interfere with his continuously trying to improve his ability to overcome the paralysis of his legs. With Mother's help, he aroused himself by taking on various nonpolitical chores. He undertook the presidency of the Boy Scouts foundation, the presidency of the American Construction Council, the chairmanship of the American Legion Campaign, and a number of other nonpolitical activities.

By the time the summer of 1922 rolled around, he became active in the campaign of Governor Alfred E. Smith for re-election. That election brought about a new development in Mother's life. Louis Howe persuaded her that she should take to the campaign trail and actively make speeches for Governor Smith. This was extremely awkward for Mother. In the first place, she had never made a campaign speech. She was badly equipped physically for public speaking because she had a rather high-pitched voice, and when she became nervous, she had a tendency to become very shrill. The net result of this made for a disastrous delivery. The first speech she ever made, she learned by heart, and the delivery was so poor that Louis Howe took to coaching her. He painstakingly set out to have her speak in a voice several octaves lower than she was accustomed to. He slowed down her delivery so that she could control her voice when she became nervous. Gradually, as the campaign progressed, she began to learn the fundamentals of good public speaking. She was to work hard and long over many years on this new facet of her career. In her later years, she became one of the great women lecturers who could hold an audience of thousands spellbound, concentrating on her every word.

The second awkward experience for Mother in the 1922 campaign was the fact that her first cousin, Colonel Theodore Roosevelt, Jr., was the Republican candidate for the governorship of New York that year. He was the son of President Theodore Roosevelt, her uncle. He had succeeded Father in 1921 as assistant secretary of the navy, and he had had a very distinguished war record in the army during World War I. Mother had always had a great deal of affection for her side of the Roosevelt family, and this was the first time that she had found that being married to a Democratic-oriented husband could cause her embarrassment in her relationship with her own side of the family. But her overriding desire to help Father regain his active pursuit of his own career was all important, even if it meant that she had to campaign actively against her own first cousin.

Her efforts paid off. Al Smith won reelection, and Father shortly became involved in promoting the New York governor for the Democratic nomination to the presidency in 1924. So much was his interest aroused that he was spending more and more time and effort in trying to rehabilitate the use of his legs, and in the process he was improving his overall physique to an astonishing degree. He was a tall man, but he had always been very slender. Since the polio had struck, he had built his upper torso to where his chest expanded to more than fifty inches, from a norm of forty-six inches, and his forearms and biceps became so muscled that he could lift his entire body by grabbing an overhead bar or rings to maneuver with ease in any way that he wanted.

Mother had won the first great triumph of her life. My father was no longer a man who believed that his life was over. He wanted to go forth and challenge the world, no matter the handicaps. Mother had won her first great battle of wills with her mother-in-law. Her husband was entering into the second great period of his life, and she was the one responsible.

Rebuilding
and New Ventures

The year 1924 marked the true reentry of Franklin Delano Roosevelt into active participation in the Democratic national struggle. That summer the Democratic party held its national convention in Madison Square Garden, New York. Father was running the campaign of Al Smith to obtain the Democratic nomination. When the convention opened, Mother took an active part in trying to get resolutions adopted regarding the rights of women, and she tried desperately to get women recognized more prominently in party councils. Mother was to relate later an amusing side remark, dropped by a famous humorist. She sat knitting throughout the convention, suffering with the heat, and wished it would end. She heard rumors of all kinds of maneuvers and all the different things that the men were talking about drifted her way.

One day she caught her first glimpse of Will Rogers when he wandered by the box and asked her, "Knitting in the names of the future victims of the guillotine?" She felt like saying that she was almost ready to call any punishment down on the heads of those who could not bring the convention to a close.

Finally, in spite of all that could be done, in spite of a really

fine nominating speech by Father and the persuasion and influence of many other people in the convention, Al Smith lost the
nomination. Father stepped gracefully out of the political picture, though he did make one or two speeches for John W.
Davis, the Democratic presidential nominee.

And so ended the early phases of the education of Eleanor
Roosevelt both in life and in politics.

After this political denouement, Father devoted every effort
to rebuilding his law practice in partnership with Basil O'Connor. The firm of Roosevelt and O'Connor, located at 120
Broadway, just a block away from Wall Street, prospered. At
the same time, Father redoubled his efforts to improve the use
of his paralyzed legs. For several years after he had first been
stricken, he had found it very beneficial to go south during the
winter months. He bought a houseboat in Florida, and he
would take one or two trips during the cold months for extended cruises through the Florida Keys and up and down the
east and west coasts of Florida. He had a passion for deep-sea
fishing, and the warm waters enabled him to exercise his legs
over extended hours of swimming. And in the early 1920s,
through a friend, George Foster Peabody, he heard of a resort in
Georgia that had mineral hot springs flowing out of the ground.
He heard that the Indians in bygone years had flocked to bathe
in these waters and that they had remarkable curative powers.
The place was known as Warm Springs, Georgia. It was a
seedy, run-down resort where the landed gentry of Atlanta
used to travel to take the baths in the days before and after the
Civil War. Father visited the spa and became very excited about
its possibilities for bringing back the use of his legs.

Mother encouraged all these efforts of his, and occasionally
she would join him on the Florida boating excursions. She had
never been able to enjoy deep-sea fishing or swimming, and
when she did go along, however infrequently, she would spend
hours at a time knitting sweaters, socks, and scarves for her

friends and family. This was a habit she had acquired when she was growing up, and she continued to knit and do needlepoint throughout her entire life. She never traveled anywhere without taking along her knitting bag, and every sedentary moment of relaxation was spent knitting away on her latest project. All who knew Mother came to recognize that her hands were continuously occupied with knitting chores, whether she was relaxing or carrying on an important conversation.

She recalled in her memoirs her joy and sadness in joining Father for the Thanksgiving celebration at Warm Springs. After Father discovered Warm Springs, he had spread the word about the curative powers of the warm waters, and many children suffering from infantile paralysis flocked to the waters seeking an improvement in their condition. Every Thanksgiving, he would gather them all together to celebrate. These gatherings made a deep impression upon my mother. She wrote, "There seemed so much happiness in the children's faces, but the complete gallantry of all the patients always brought a choke to my throat. Some of them were on stretchers, some in wheelchairs, some on crutches. Some hoped to get well, many faced permanent handicaps, but all were cheerful that one evening at least."

Mother busied herself during these years in the twenties with her domestic responsibilities with which she was becoming quite adept. In the early years of her marriage, she had had an independent inherited income that varied between $5,000 and $8,000 per year. From the outset, she had contributed from her own income to the costs of running the household, and with servants and all, Mother and Father lived comfortably, if not luxuriously, on $600 per month. Of course, as the years went by, and as the children went off to school, the costs increased and it became necessary for Father to contribute more to the family budget. Mother's trust fund was always handled by older relatives in her family, and, unfortunately, the control eventually passed into the hands of a New York bank. In the

Great Depression of 1929, she suddenly found that all of her investments, which had previously been in blue-chip securities, had been sold during the boom years of the twenties and reinvested in the stock of the bank that handled her trust. When the Depression hit, the stock of that bank plummeted in value, and her earnings per year from this source became almost nonexistent.

It was during this period that Mother continued to expand her interests in state political activities. She also found that she could be more and more effective as a public speaker. Her expanding role in the organizations that she worked for meant that she attended more strategy meetings and her clear, analytical mind started to assert itself. She assumed more and more of a leadership role.

In the middle twenties, Mother formed a close relationship with two of the workers in the women's division of the Democratic State Committee, Nancy Cook and Marion Dickerman. For years she had chafed over the extended periods that the whole family spent at Hyde Park. She was so used to running her own household that when we were all at Hyde Park, she felt like an outsider who was visiting. That was because Hyde Park was the exclusive domain of her mother-in-law. If she had, even in a minor way, interfered in the domestic operation of the household at Hyde Park, Granny would have been furious. So one day Mother approached Father about the possibility of her being able to have a separate little hideaway cottage where she could retreat and get away from the domination of her mother-in-law. She was quite frank in expressing her frustrations to Father. He not only understood and agreed with her, but also entered into the project with her of building the little cottage beside a brook, where they often went to picnic during the first years after Father was paralyzed. The brook was called Val-Kill and so the cottage was christened Val-Kill cottage. They hired an architect from Georgia, and Father was the contractor on the

Mother with her closest friends, Marion Dickerman and Nancy Cook
FRANKLIN D. ROOSEVELT LIBRARY

job. Both of them worked with enormous enthusiasm and a shared sense of accomplishment in completing this charming little stone house with its swimming pool alongside.

Soon after the cottage was completed, Mother and Father conceived a new idea. Father had always had an interest in finding an industry that could be developed in a rural area, such as ours at Hyde Park, that could furnish an occupation for some of the young men who would otherwise leave the farms. By getting them in an industry which would yield them a fairly good income during slack periods on the farm, he thought one could keep these young people working steadily so that the standard of farm development in the area could be raised. Mother explained that Father had a great love for the soil and wanted to see it develop, but he realized that many of the farmers around them had a difficult time holding their young sons on the land because the return for hard and strenuous work was meager. His interest in the new enterprise was therefore in the training and employment of young men in the vicinity.

So, a factory was built adjacent to the little stone cottage. Nancy Cook was asked to run the factory. She chose it to be a furniture factory, making reproductions of Early American furniture. A Scandinavian cabinetmaker was employed to assist Nancy Cook in teaching the local men their new craft. The furniture was all made by hand. The reproductions were chosen with the help and cooperation of the Metropolitan Museum of Art and the Hartford Museum. For a number of years, this factory grew and prospered.

At the same time, Mother became interested in another enterprise, which had been initiated by Marion Dickerman. Miss Dickerman was an assistant principal, and then the principal, of a private girls' school in New York, called the Todhunter School. This school admitted girls from the primary grades through high school. Mother became associated with the school in 1927, after Marion Dickerman had bought the school from its founder, Miss Todhunter. Mother started by giving courses in American history, and in English and American literature, to the older girls in the school. Later on, she added a course in current events. She invested money in this enterprise and became a part owner. It was quite clear that during these years in the twenties, Mother was developing enormous energy and ability to cope with many diverse activities.

All of this did not lessen her concern over giving her offspring proper attention as a parent. She had felt during the years leading up to Father's illness and months of recuperation that the three older children had not enjoyed a sufficient amount of her personal attention. She was determined that the two youngest, Franklin, Jr., and John, would not suffer from neglect. As a result, she planned on taking the two boys on a long summer camping trip. Nancy Cook and Marion Dickerman started out one day with Mother, Franklin, Jr., and John on the carefully planned outing. They were going up through New York State and into Canada for a leisurely trip around the Maritime Provinces.

The first few days of camping out in scenic places went smoothly, but very soon the two boys started to get bored. Day after day, driving in the car from one scenic spot to another and stopping during the noon hour for a picnic alongside the road did not appeal to the active youngsters. The grown-ups were satisfied to make camp, quietly enjoy the scenery, and rest up for the next day's journey. Slowly, the docile and obedient youngsters started to become more and more obstreperous. They would go off on their own at each new camping site to find a swimming hole or a rocky hill to climb. They wouldn't turn up for meals when they were supposed to and Miss Cook and Miss Dickerman started to complain about the disobedience of the young. At each new outburst from the older women, the boys reacted by inventing new pranks to play, to make them more annoyed. Mother tried hard to keep peace. She understood the exuberance of her children, but she could also understand the frazzled nerves of her women companions. She knew that they weren't used to a rowdy family. Pretty soon, Nancy Cook and Marion Dickerman came to a decision. They wanted to cut the camping trip short. Mother was very distressed. She had entered into the outing with such high hopes of having a delightful opportunity to do something with her two youngest children that would be a pleasant memory for them, and she realized that it had been a disastrous failure. Sadly, the trip came to an end, and Franklin, Jr., and John returned to their more accustomed summer activities.

5

From Albany
to Washington

In the summer of 1928, Franklin Roosevelt had again agreed to place Governor Alfred E. Smith in nomination for the presidency at the Democratic Convention, which was to be held in Houston, Texas. He traveled to the convention by train, and I accompanied him. At the convention he made a truly inspiring speech on behalf of Governor Smith, and in spite of the fact that the convention was held in a southern state where considerable anti-Catholic sentiment existed, he was successful in securing the nomination on the Democratic ticket for Al Smith, a Catholic.

After the convention, I proceeded on west to follow my own pursuits, and Father headed back to Warm Springs, Georgia, to continue his therapy. He charged Mother with the responsibility of representing him at the State Convention in Rochester, New York, that fall. According to Mother's own account, Governor Smith and Mr. John J. Raskob, then the chairman of the Democratic National Committee, put a lot of pressure on her to persuade her husband that he should accept the nomination for governor of the state of New York in order to help the national ticket in that state. Mother refused to use any pressure on Father, and when they put in a call on her behalf to Father, he told her that he would not have spoken to anyone else on the telephone. So Mother adroitly answered that she had called only because Governor Smith and Mr. Raskob had begged her to. She told him that she was turning the telephone over to Governor Smith because she had to catch a train. Then she ran from the room. Evidently, Al Smith was very persuasive. The next morning, when Mother bought a newspaper, she read that her husband had been persuaded to accept the nomination.

In November, Governor Alfred E. Smith was defeated for the presidency and lost New York State. Franklin Roosevelt was elected governor by a very slim margin of 25,000 votes. At this point, Mother suddenly realized that we were again cast into a public role. Life would not be as private, and my parents' movements would have to be adapted to the requirements of their public position.

When Mother moved with Father to Albany on January 1, 1929, she was not very happy with the decor of the executive mansion. She found it overpoweringly formal and stuffy. It was filled with gilt furniture, gilt-framed mirrors and pictures, and vast amounts of red velvet curtains at the enormous windows. Outside of a small study downstairs, Mother made little attempt to change the appearance of the major rooms on the ground floor. But on the second floor, where most of the bedrooms were located, she tried to make them airy and comfortable.

Her own life during those governorship years was a full one. In her teaching, she had for the first time a job that she did not wish to give up. This led to her planning to spend a few days every week in New York City, except during the school vacation. So Mother escaped from Albany as often as she could during the week. She leaned on Marguerite "Missy" LeHand, Father's secretary, to look after the household duties at the executive mansion. She had come to have a great affection for Missy because she believed that her wholehearted devotion to her husband was very beneficial.

She did travel, during the summer of 1929, with Franklin, Jr., and John to Europe. On that trip, she showed them the fronts over which our soldiers had fought in World War I. She also took them to some of the cemeteries where our men had been interred. She took them, particularly, to visit the grave of her first cousin, Quentin Roosevelt. He was a son of President Theodore Roosevelt and had flown as a pilot in World War I. He had been shot down and killed toward the latter part of the conflict. She remarked later about that trip that her son Franklin said to her one day, "This is a funny country, there are only boys our age and old men coming out of the fields. There don't seem to be any men of Father's age." That was simply another proof that the war had taken from France a heavy toll of young men from 1914 to 1918.

In 1930, a new campaign for the governorship took place. Father was reelected in an easy campaign by a landslide vote. This made Franklin Roosevelt an important possible candidate for president of the United States in 1932. Mother's attention to Father's welfare was shown by an incident that took place during Father's second term as governor. There was a governors' conference in Richmond, Virginia, and President Herbert Hoover invited all the governors to the White House to dine. Mother was familiar with the way in which guests had to stand in the East Room at a state dinner before they were received by the president and his wife, so she was worried about Father, who had to have somebody's arm and a cane. In addition, he became tired if he stood without support for any length of time. They arrived a little ahead of time, since they knew they would have to walk rather slowly down the main hall to get into line, and then they would wait for a long time. The president and Mrs. Hoover did not appear. Father was twice offered a chair,

Father takes the oath of office for his second term as governor of New
York State, 1930.   FRANKLIN D. ROOSEVELT LIBRARY

but he thought that if he showed any weakness someone might
make an adverse political story out of it, so he refused each
time. It seemed as though he were being deliberately put
through an endurance test, but he managed the whole evening
very well, though the half-hour wait before the president appeared was an ordeal.

Finally the time approached for the Democratic party to
choose its candidate to run against President Hoover in the fall
of 1932. For two years, Mother had assisted Louis Howe and
Jim Farley in the building of a grass roots political organization

Father and Mother in Columbus, Ohio, on one of their many campaign trips in 1932, when Father ran for the presidency for the first time   WIDE WORLD

in every state of the union. In spite of Father's enormous popularity throughout the country, when the convention finally met, he lacked the necessary votes to secure the nomination. Some very astute political horse-trading went on behind the scenes at the Chicago convention. The delegations from California and Texas were crucial to a Roosevelt nomination. Under the direction of Louis Howe, Jim Farley managed to persuade the California Democratic leader, William Gibbs McAdoo, and his mentor, William Randolph Hearst, to swing the votes of Texas and California in return for Father's agreeing to select John Nance Garner as his running mate for vice president. As soon as this political trade had been made, the nomination was secure. Then, a new departure in political tradition was decided upon. Previously the presidential and vice-presidential nominees were visited in their homes following the convention to be notified of their nomination, and then they made gracious acceptance speeches. The Roosevelt strategy was quite the opposite. No president or presidential nominee had ever flown in the course of duty. Franklin Roosevelt chartered a commercial airliner, a Ford Tri-Motor, to fly from Albany to Chicago, direct to the convention. So it was that Father, Mother, Johnny, and I, together with a number of other members of the staff, embarked from the Albany airport on a blustery, stormy day.

Fighting rain and headwinds, the plane landed in Buffalo, New York, to refuel, and then flew on to Chicago. Most of the party, including Mother, was violently airsick. Father remained engrossed in rewriting parts of his acceptance speech. As we arrived in Chicago, the sun burst through the clouds, and we came down at the airport to be greeted by thousands of well-wishers. Everyone was bundled into waiting limousines, and with screaming sirens coming from the police motorcycle escort, we were whisked to the convention.

With Mother standing at his side, Father stood at the podium as the convention went wild. He delivered a stirring and hard-hitting acceptance speech that effectively set the tone for the coming campaign. President Hoover, running for reelection, was gravely handicapped by the ever deepening depression that had followed the stock market crash in 1929. The country was highly demoralized, and between 25 percent and 30 percent of the work force of America was unemployed. The Roosevelt campaign offered hope to a discouraged nation. The November election in 1932 was an easy victory for Franklin Roosevelt.

My mother faced a new challenge far more complicated than any other challenge that she had been called upon before to face. We have to remember that although she had dedicated herself to the furtherance of her husband's career, at the same time she had been determined in her efforts to broaden the scope of her own life and abilities. Now that she had helped Father to obtain the highest public office in the land, she herself had taken on a two-fold commitment. First, she would have to assist him in his task to the limit of her ability, and second, she would have to accept the role of first lady with all of its social and public implications. Many of her personal enterprises would have to be curtailed.

President's Partner

When Franklin Roosevelt was elected to the presidency, our country was in the depths of the worst depression in memory. Millions of people were out of work. Factories were closing in every section of the land. Farmers received so little for their crops and their livestock that they could no longer afford to operate their farms. People and businesses were going bankrupt right and left.

As the time for the inauguration on March 4, 1933, approached, it became quite evident to Mother and Father that an enormous crisis was about to engulf them. They recognized all too clearly that if this new administration was to succeed, it would have to move with lightning speed to remove the despair that was sweeping the country and reverse the complete breakdown of the economy that was rapidly approaching.

So it was that on inauguration day, Franklin Roosevelt traveled to the Capitol, accompanied by his wife and his entire family. There he delivered an inaugural address that was carried by radio to practically every household in this country: "This Nation asks for action, and action now. Our greatest primary task is to put people to work." Everyone listened and everyone was electrified. Excerpts from that speech became engraved in the minds and hearts of his listeners. After the speech, Father and Mother returned to the White House and prepared to review the traditional inaugural parade as it passed down Pennsylvania Avenue, past the reviewing stand, in front of the White House. There was a mood of excitement and hope that imbued not only the participants in the parade but all the hundreds of thousands of visitors and Washingtonians who lined the streets that afternoon.

That evening, Father and Mother had decided to have a family dinner. Only members of the family who were related as first cousins or closer were to be invited. One incident was to mar the evening for Mother. Alice Longworth, President Theodore Roosevelt's daughter and Mother's first cousin, was naturally invited. She was famed throughout Washington society for her caustic tongue, and she had always denigrated her cousin Eleanor as being an inept and bumbling personality. On this evening, she went out of her way to let Eleanor know that in her opinion the White House would suffer in the coming years while she filled the role of first lady. With this sole exception, all the cousins, both Democratic and Republican, cheered enthusiastically the takeover by Franklin and Eleanor Roosevelt as president and first lady of the land.

The inaugural day had scarcely passed when Mother and Father were plunged into their exciting new roles. Almost immediately, Father was faced with the fact that many of the banks were going to fail. Hundreds were closing every day. He quickly declared a bank holiday and closed all the banks before there could be any more failures, and he asked for vast emergency executive powers to deal with the chaotic economic conditions. The Congress acquiesced. Meanwhile, there was so much to do and so little time to do it in that Father needed accurate and quick reports from various sectors of our country as to exact conditions and how bad the crisis was in all areas. The information coming in was uniformly hysterical. It was hard to get solid facts on which to act.

Mother was constantly traveling. One day she would be in the coal fields of West Virginia, next she was visiting the steel mills in Pennsylvania, then Father would send her through the grain fields of the Middle West. On another day she would find herself in the hot and dusty cotton fields of the South. Always she asked questions of workers and farmers, factory operators and union leaders, and always she made it a point to visit the wives and children she met in every part of America. As she gathered her information, every night she would sit down at her portable typewriter and peck out long reports to Father of what she had learned that day. Sometimes in the course of a day, she would run across emergency situations, where some action had to be taken within a matter of hours or days. Then she would communicate by telephone.

The days passed into weeks, and the weeks became months, and the steady flow of information that Mother was sending back to Father in the White House began to help him in formulating programs that would help people bring order back into their lives. Jobs were created, the banks were reopened, people's deposits were insured, foreclosure of homes and farms was stopped. Loan assistance was provided for farmers, factories reopened as more people could support their families and could commence again to buy staple goods and the other necessities for the home.

As Mother continued her travels, she was also reporting back to Father serious dislocations that existed in our economic life. She made him aware of the sweatshops that still existed in the garment industry, where women and children were still used and paid pitifully low wages for long hours of toil. She reported that in many areas of our country, first- and second-generation immigrants were employed by heavy industry at low wages and long hours. She wrote back to him how the Negroes throughout the South were discriminated against. They

On a trip to California, Mother meets the children of migrant workers. UNITED PRESS INTERNATIONAL

were kept in a state of second-class citizenry by being denied equal educational benefits and being paid wages that were a fraction of those of their white counterparts. All the inequities that existed in our American way of life were forcefully brought home to Mother. Gradually her reports to Father became the stimulus of the new administration's developing policy. Franklin Roosevelt christened this program the New Deal.

The partnership of Mother and Father had wrought a revolution in the United States. The people of the land had come to believe and trust their new leader, who talked to them frequently in their own homes in what he called his radio fireside chats. These same people came to expect the appearance of the first lady in their communities and in their homes. They welcomed the opportunity to relay their problems to her, knowing that if there was anything that could be done for them by their government, it would be done quickly and with no red tape.

Probably the most interesting way in which Mother's and Father's partnership was organized was evidenced by the team that they installed to assist them. Father and Mother brought Missy LeHand and Louis Howe to live in the White House. These two acted as liaison between the activities of each of the partners. In addition to her many travels, Mother had to act as official hostess at the White House, while Father was inundated with the demands of the presidency. So oftentimes, personal contact became difficult. Missy and Louis were more and more frequently called upon to carry messages back and forth. It is interesting to note that in those hectic days when the president was receiving thousands of letters a day, the first lady was often called upon to wade through as many as two thousand letters a day. She made a point of answering every communication, and she had one secretary who handled all of this. Her constant companion for many years of her life, Malvina "Tommy" Thompson, performed this task as well as looking after her personal correspondence with friends and family. Mother's only other assistant was Mrs. James (Edith) Helm, the widow of

With her secretaries, Malvina Thompson and Edith Helm, Mother
answers one of the thousands of letters received daily in the White
House.   JACKIE MARTIN / FRANKLIN D. ROOSEVELT LIBRARY

Mother and I in Los Angeles, June 1933   FRANKLIN D. ROOSEVELT
LIBRARY

an admiral, who handled all of her social duties as first lady.

Today, it is hard for me to realize that in addition to all of these aforementioned duties, Mother kept up a constant, long-hand correspondence with all of her children and she took plenty of time to visit with her children and grandchildren, when they visited the White House. During her travels around the country, if she was going to be within five hundred miles of a child, she would make a point to plan a short visit.

In addition, Mother had to run the staff of the White House. She and Father had a strict budget within which they had to operate. In spite of this, the president's salary and allowances from the government never quite seemed to cover their yearly budget. Unfortunately, they felt that the office of the president of the United States had to be carried on in such a manner that the people would be proud of the entire way in which the White House was operating. Therefore, it became necessary for them to borrow, rather extensively, from Sarah Delano Roosevelt, Father's mother. As a result, in the twelve years that our family occupied the White House, Granny subsidized the presidency to the tune of about $100,000 per year.

Mother tried in other ways to help out the family exchequer. She entered into a contract to write a column, six days a week, entitled "My Day." This column was syndicated widely to many newspapers throughout the country. It was easy for her to write it because she related to her readers what she did each day of her peripatetic existence. Later, she was also to add to this a monthly column which she wrote for the *Ladies' Home Journal*. In this column, she answered many questions from those who wrote to her. Much of the income she derived from her writings, and later supplemented by income from lectures, went to a list of charities. Her quiet devotion to a long list of charitable causes has been little known to the general public.

7

In the Public Eye

The emergence of Mother as a recognizable figure to the people of the United States was a mixed blessing. She had never before been a controversial figure, but as she went around the country, people started to pay attention to what she said and how she acted. Pretty soon columnists like Westbrook Pegler started directing vitriolic insults at her. She began to realize that her opinion as expressed in the press and through her writings and from the lecture podium were creating for her a great deal of notoriety. Always in the past, she had been in the background, but now she had to live her life in the glare of the public spotlight. Her every action was noted and either praised or criticized. She herself as first lady had become as much a public figure as her husband, the president. This became a sometimes onerous burden. She was not afraid to express her deep-seated convictions and principles in public. What she did object to was the total invasion of her privacy. There was never a moment that the news media was not recording her goings and comings and her every action.

Mother really was a very private person, and I think that

this, more than anything else, caused her to look forward eagerly to the day when Father no longer would be president. She knew that it was inevitable that he would want to serve a second term, and so she resigned herself to the probability that she would have to be first lady of the land for eight years. Much earlier she had written about the gossip and rumors and, yes, even slander that circulated around public figures. In 1932, during the presidential campaign, she had been upset by a rumor that the Republicans planned to issue a statement claiming that infantile paralysis was a progressive disease, which eventually affected the brain. She also noted that her mother-in-law was never happy about the gossip and rumors concerning her and her son and her grandsons. Mother wrote in her autobiography, "Disagreeable letters upset her very much and the statement that she was paid by the government for the use of her house at Hyde Park as a summer White House distressed her above everything. She was proud of her home and extremely happy when her son and his family and friends could be with her, and nothing would have induced her to accept money from any source. In any case, there was at no time a suggestion of government pay, and after her death her son continued to pay the expenses of the house and grounds out of his own pocket."

In Father's case even his little dog, Fala, came in for his share of false accusations. I remember all too well a discussion that was held between Father and Mother on one occasion when Westbrook Pegler had written a particularly nasty article about Mother. She had clipped it out of the paper and had brought it into Father one evening in his study. I could tell that she could barely control her anger, and the tears were very close to her eyes. She thrust the clipping in front of Father and said, "Franklin, read this! Isn't there something I can do about the lies and innuendos which that evil man is continuously printing about me? I'd like to do something to shut him up."

"Wait a minute, dear," Father replied, "let me just read this article first." He adjusted his reading glasses and read through the article. After he finished reading, he laid it aside and looked up at Mother. Concern was in his expression as he paused and then answered, "Eleanor, I know just how you feel. I feel the same way every time I read these despicable stories that are written about you. Actually you know, when they print stories that are derogatory about you or the children, they are only trying to get at me. Long ago I developed a thick hide and I'm now impervious to any nonsense that they dig up about me. I realize that for you and the children, it is much more difficult. I have only one piece of advice to give you. Remember that these people who attack you are nothing more than low-life skunks, and it's wrong for any of us to get in a pissing contest with a skunk. You just have to learn to ignore these attacks and continue on doing what you have to do."

In spite of the strenuous schedule that Mother kept up in traveling around the country at the behest of Father, she quickly organized the White House itself from a household standpoint and became adjusted to meeting the social obligations that a president's wife has to maintain. She did this with the aid of her two secretaries and Mrs. Henrietta Nesbitt, whom she had brought to the White House as housekeeper.

Mother was the first wife of a president to institute regular press conferences. When she initiated these press conferences, she realized that she should not trespass on her husband's prerogatives, that national and international news must be handled by him. She felt that some of her own activities might be of interest, but it was new and untried ground and she was feeling her way with some trepidation.

Early on, in the first year in office, Father felt that the economic and political situation in the world made it necessary for him to establish contacts with the leaders of other countries. Mother described the reception that Father worked out to make them feel that the United States recognized the importance of their government. If the guests arrived in the afternoon, there would be tea for the entire party; afterward all but the most important guests went to a hotel or to their own embassy. Later, Blair House, across from Pennsylvania Avenue, was acquired by the government and furnished for the use of important visitors. The head of a government would spend one night in the White House, accompanied by his wife, if she was with him. There usually was a state dinner with conversation or music afterward. The following morning, Father and his guests would often have another talk, before the guests went over to Blair House or to their embassy.

During the first year, Ramsay MacDonald of England and the prime minister of Canada came to stay. Edouard Herriot, the French statesman, also arrived in Washington. The Italian, German, Chinese, and Japanese missions were entertained. The governor general of the Philippines brought with him Manuel Quezon, the top Philippine government representative. Others who received special White House attention were the prime minister of New Zealand and His Highness Prince Ras Desta Dember, the special ambassador of the emperor of Ethiopia. From our own hemisphere, the president of Panama paid a visit and a stag dinner was held for the Brazilian delegation; a special ambassador from the Argentine was received; and the Mexican and Brazilian envoys were guests.

These events have been mentioned here only to give some idea of the enormous vitality and gusto that Mother brought to her job of serving Father in accomplishing the task which he had set for himself by becoming president of the United States. In spite of Mother's constant activities during those White House years, she never once failed to keep in close touch with her five children. When all of us were away in various parts of the country, it was rare indeed that she did not manage to write each and every child a long and breezy letter, keeping us advised of just what Father and she were doing and how all the members were faring within the family.

8

First Year
in the White House

In the first year of Mother's residence in the White House, she found out that being the wife of the president of the United States was not quite as simple a task, nor as enjoyable a position, as an outsider might think. First of all, there was the fact that the Secret Service expected to have one of their agents traveling with her wherever she went. This custom struck Mother as completely unnecessary and ludicrous. She flatly refused to travel around the country accompanied by a Secret Service agent. In desperation, the Secret Service finally convinced her that she should carry a small revolver with her at all times when she was driving around the country alone.

In the summer of 1933, she attempted to learn how to use the weapon and she practiced target shooting until she finally learned how to hit the target. She was convinced that she would never use the weapon to shoot a human being. In later years the Secret Service realized that she kept the weapon with her only when she was traveling alone in her car. At all other times, she was completely vulnerable to an attack. The Secret Service then came up with a brilliant new idea. They brought her a small cylindrical object that looked like a fat pocket pen. They told her that she could carry this in her purse. It was a gas gun, which could be used at close quarters and would temporarily blind or choke anyone that it was fired at. Years after she had been instructed to carry this with her, I happened to be rummaging through her purse. I don't really remember what the reason was for my doing this; maybe I was looking to borrow some change or something of that sort. In any event, I ran across this fat little pen and, holding it up, I asked Mother, "What is it for?" She replied that it was a gas gun. So I looked at it curiously and asked her, "How does this thing work?" She replied, "I haven't the faintest idea. I've been carrying it for a number of years and I've neglected to ask the Secret Service how to fire it."

This was typical of Mother's attitude. She approached life believing that she was too unimportant to attract the attention of an assassin, and even if someone were to be deranged to the point of attempting to kill her, she was completely fatalistic. If someone suggested that it was possible, she would merely shrug her shoulders and comment, "Well, in that event, I suppose it would be time for me to go to heaven and it certainly wouldn't be any great loss."

Her role as an observer of the national scene developed slowly during the first presidential year. After trips which either she or Father had taken, they both tried to arrange for an uninterrupted meal so that each could hear the other's whole story while it was still fresh. That she became, as the years went by, a better reporter and a better observer, was largely owing to the fact that Father's questions covered such a wide range. She found herself obliged to notice everything. For instance, when she returned from a trip around the Gaspé, he wanted to know not only what kind of fishing and hunting was possible in that area but what the life of the fisherman was, how he lived, what the farms were like, how the houses were built, what types of schools were available, and whether they were controlled by the church. When she mentioned Maine, he wanted to know

My parents in the president's study in the White House during Father's first year in office   FRANKLIN D. ROOSEVELT LIBRARY

about everything she had seen on the farms she visited, the kinds of homes and the types of people, how the Indians seemed to be getting on and where they came from. Father never praised her for her reporting. She realized, however, that he would not question her so closely if he were not interested, and she decided this was the best way she could help him, outside of running the house, which was soon organized and running itself under Mrs. Nesbitt.

Soon Mother was making more and more trips at Father's request. The autumn of 1933 found her investigating the conditions that existed in coal mining areas of West Virginia. She related a story at the White House dinner table one night after returning from her tour of the coal mining areas. "In a company house I visited where the people had evidently seen better days, the man showed me his weekly pay slips. A small amount had been deducted toward his bill at the company store and for his rent and for oil for his mine lamp. These deductions left him less than a dollar in cash each week. There were six children in the family, and they acted as though they were afraid of strangers. I noticed a bowl on the table filled with scraps, the kind that you or I might give to a dog, and I saw children, evidently looking for their noonday meal, take a handful out of that bowl and go out munching. That was all they had to eat. As I went out, two of the children had gathered enough courage to stand by the door, the little boy holding a white rabbit in his arms. It was evident that it was a most cherished pet. The little girl was thin and scrawny, and had a gleam in her eyes as she looked at her brother. She said, 'He thinks we are not going to eat it, but we are.' And at that, the small boy fled down the road clutching the rabbit closer than ever." Present at that dinner was William C. Bullitt, then the United States ambassador to France, and he sent Mother a check the next day, saying he hoped it might help to keep the rabbit alive.

As a result of Mother's trips, and because of Father's realization that fast action must be taken to alleviate the terrible conditions in every corner of the country, a program was begun to assist the plight of the miners in West Virginia. The Civilian Conservation Corps was created a month after Father entered the White House to assist youngsters who were graduating from high school and college but could find no employment anywhere. Mother wrote about the forestry camps, saying, "Franklin realized that the boys should be given some other kind of education as well, but it had to be subordinate to the

As first lady, Mother traveled throughout the United States and reported back to Father on living and working conditions during the Depression. Here she is about to enter a coal mine in Neffs, Ohio.   UNITED PRESS INTERNATIONAL

day's labor required of them. The Civilian Conservation Corps had a triple value: It gave the boys a chance to see different parts of their own country, and to learn to do a good day's work in the open, which benefited them physically; also it gave them a cash income, part of which went home to their families. This helped the morale both of the boys themselves and of the people at home. The idea was his own contribution to the vast

[*63*]

scheme of relief rehabilitation planning." The National Recovery Administration, the Public Works Administration, the Civil Works Administration and the Tennessee Valley Authority were a few of the myriads of job programs that emerged in those early days.

The banks during the early part of the new administration were failing at such a rapid rate that the entire fiscal structure of the country was about to collapse. The bank holiday closed all of the banks and gave the government an opportunity to restructure the whole national financial picture, so that when the banks reopened, confidence was restored and deposits returned. Such programs as the Federal Deposit Insurance Corporation came into being to insure individual deposits up to $10,000. Today they are insured up to $100,000.

As the year 1933 came to an end, the people of the United States breathed more confidently. Hope replaced fear, and while times were still very tough for the great majority, people looked forward to the coming years with much more confidence. Father and Mother began to feel that they were making progress in the tremendous struggle that had faced them in their first nine months in the White House. Each day that passed brought more tasks to be faced, but they were gaining confidence. Critics of their actions were beginning to emerge. There were many who considered that they were bringing communism, or, at the least, socialism, into the democratic system. The rich and secure felt threatened, but the mainstream of the American people looked upon their new president and his first lady as parental figures. They felt a kinship to the couple in the White House, because they knew that this couple had their interests at heart. When a fireside chat was scheduled to be on the radio on a given day, scarcely a home in America was not tuned in with the entire family gathered around to hear what new remedies and plans were in the offing to make their lives more abundant.

Royal Visitors

The years 1934 and 1935 seemed to Mother to be the most peaceful years of any that she spent in the White House. The reforms instituted at the beginning of Father's term in office were beginning to put the country back on an even keel. The age-old animosities that had existed between management and labor, and between the president and the Congress, seemed to be much less apparent. Mother continued her tireless travels, visiting rural schools as well as urban schools. Her trips included the slums that existed in every part of the United States. She was horrified at the conditions that she found people living in in Puerto Rico and the Virgin Islands. Her efforts to alleviate these problems got results. Federal officials moved in to all of the slum areas and started instituting new programs to improve the lot of the people. By early 1936, every section of the United States was showing a distinct improvement in the way of life for the people.

The spring of 1936 left a great gap in Mother's and Father's life. Louis Howe, the gnomelike man who had been their most intimate friend and adviser for over twenty-five years, finally was overcome by his long-standing frail health. He had practically lived with them both through all of their travails. He had had his own room in the White House, and he was one of Father's closest advisers. He had been completely responsible for Mother's emergence as a public figure of unflagging energy. Finally, his weakened heart and emphysema forced him to the hospital. Soon thereafter, word was received that he had died. I don't think anybody was ever as sorely missed by my parents as he was. Mother completely relied upon his judgment and advice. He did more to shape her understanding of people's needs and to instruct her on how best she could help in alleviating the misfortunes of others than anyone else. He helped my father to gain the insight and the compassion to realize that it was the responsibility of government to look after the welfare of all our nation's people. It was he who implanted in my father's mind the fact that the United States was a symbol of greatness and freedom to most of the people on this earth. He believed strongly that the United States was the only nation that could promote and achieve freedom for all of the people scattered throughout the world living in suppression and deprivation. Neither of my parents ever forgot the lessons that he taught them.

The summer of 1936 found Father running for a second term. That election in November proved to be the most decisive election that had ever taken place in the annals of American history. Every state in the union, with the exception of two—Maine and Vermont—was carried by the Democratic candidate. Mother seemed to enjoy the winning of this election much more than any of the other victory celebrations in which she had partaken over the years. I think the reason she felt this way was that she realized Father's success was in large part achieved as much by her efforts on his behalf as by those of any one other person. It must have been thrilling for her to read the hundreds of thousands of congratulatory messages which came to the White House addressed to both of them after this election. So many of them referred to her visits with them around the country. The team of Roosevelt and Roosevelt was certainly capturing the hearts of the American people.

After the election, Father began devoting more and more time to building his Good Neighbor policy in Latin America. During one of the trips that Father made Mother tried her hand at her first real lecture trip. This trip was under the auspices of the W. Colston Leigh Lecture Bureau. Mother enjoyed her first lecture trip, as she felt that she was getting a good opportunity to meet a lot of people who formed a cross-section of our population. She did remark that, as time went by, she found that people no longer considered her a mouthpiece for her husband but realized that she had a point of view of her own with which he might not at all agree. As she became more and more free in expressing her own views, she would quite often check with Father to see whether he approved of her viewpoint in a column or article. Invariably, he kept a hands-off policy and allowed her to express her own opinion without reservation. This had its own advantages for Father, because many times her views would serve as a trial balloon, and he could observe the reactions without in any way expressing agreement on his part.

One of the personal incidents of disagreement between the president and his first lady occurred in 1937. He asked his son James to come to Washington as one of his secretaries. Jimmy was delighted and accepted with alacrity. Mother expressed grave concern because she felt that Father would be attacked for nepotism and Jimmy would get into all kinds of hot water that would reflect upon Father. Mother protested vehemently to Father and told him he was selfish to bring James down to Washington. Finally, she was silenced by her husband, who said, "Why should I be deprived of my eldest son's help and the pleasure of having him with me just because I am the presi-

King George VI (*far left*) and Queen Elizabeth (*far right*) of England arrive in Washington, D.C., for an official visit in 1939.   FRANKLIN D. ROOSEVELT LIBRARY

dent?" Later when Jimmy was attacked by critics, Mother was to feel that her anxieties had been justified, even though she was very proud of the job that Jimmy did in fulfilling his duties.

The summer of 1938 marked the beginning of a series of visits from members of Europe's royal families. The crown prince and princess of Norway, and the crown prince of Denmark were among the early visitors, but by far the most interesting visitors were the king and queen of England—King

Queen Elizabeth and Mother in the car on the way from Union
Station to the White House   UNITED PRESS INTERNATIONAL

George and Queen Elizabeth. King George VI had succeeded
his brother King Edward VIII after Edward abdicated the throne
because of his love of Mrs. Wally Simpson. The abdication had
taken place in 1936. The visit of King George marked the first
time that a monarch of Great Britain had set foot in the United
States since the Revolutionary War. A great deal of protocol
and customs needed to be observed during the visit of reigning
royalty. Mother and Father had to decide whether British customs would be followed in the seating at the dinner table.

Under British protocol, the president should sit with the king to his right and the queen to his left, and the first lady would sit to the right of the king. Mother decided to disregard this custom after conferring with Father. The king would sit to the right of my mother and the queen on my father's right, and Mother and Father would follow their usual custom of sitting directly across the table from each other. After this custom was explained to the king and queen, they graciously agreed that it was much more sensible and they seemed to enjoy the arrangements that were made for them from that time on.

The king and queen's visit continued for several days, ending with a trip to Hyde Park. When they arrived, Mother met them at the door and took them to their rooms. In a short time, they were dressed and down in the library. As the king approached Father and the cocktail table, Father said, "My mother does not approve of cocktails and thinks you should have a cup of tea." The king answered, "Neither does my mother" and took a cocktail.

Another of the amusing stories concerning that visit bears repeating. Two startling things happened at dinner that caused my granny much embarrassment. Grandmother had the extra china that was needed put on a serving table that was not ordinarily used, and suddenly in the middle of dinner the serving table collapsed and the dishes clattered to the floor. Granny tried, in the best-bred tradition, to ignore it, but her step-daughter-in-law, Mrs. James Roosevelt Roosevelt, from whom she had borrowed some plates for the occasion, was heard to say to the king, "I hope none of my dishes were among those broken." As a matter of fact, the broken dishes were part of a set given to the president; none of the old family china suffered. One mishap of this kind would seem enough for an evening, but just after the family and guests were going down to the big library after dinner, there was a crash; the butler, carrying a tray of decanters, glasses, and bowls of ice, fell down the two steps leading from the hall and slid right into the library, scattering the contents of the tray over the floor and leaving a large lake of water and ice cubes at the bottom of the steps. Mother wrote about this in her column at the time because she thought it was really funny, but her mother-in-law was indignant with her for not keeping it a family secret.

The day after that nearly disastrous dinner party, Mother put on a picnic for the royal pair up at Father's unfinished "top cottage," a hilltop refuge being built to serve as a hideaway. There the king and queen ate American hotdogs for the first time and experienced a true American delicacy—smoked turkey, as well as smoked ham, cured in different parts of the United States. This informal family-style visit by the king and queen of England solidified the friendship of the two English-speaking countries, and as the royal couple stood on the rear platform of their train at the Hyde Park station, the townspeople who were gathered along the railroad tracks and on the banks of the Hudson River spontaneously burst out singing "Auld Lang Syne." Mother's thought on this occasion was "There was something incredibly moving about the scene—the river in the evening light, the voices of many people singing this old song, and the train slowly pulling out with the young couple waving goodbye. One thought of the clouds that hung over them and the worries they were going to face, and turned away and left the scene with a heavy heart."

❧ 10 ❧

Clouds of War

In 1938, Hitler started to flex his military muscles. He marched into Czechoslovakia and by the summer of 1939, he was preparing for the invasion of Poland. Neville Chamberlain, the prime minister of England, had gone to Munich to meet with Hitler and try to prevent Germany from further aggressive acts. Father and Mother both thought that Neville Chamberlain had been extremely weak in standing up to Hitler, but they felt that England had let her defenses go down so much that, perhaps, there was nothing else that the prime minister could do. Seeing Chamberlain's dilemma convinced Father that he must take steps to strengthen America's defenses.

All through 1938 and 1939, Father tried his best to avert the inevitable war that was approaching in Europe. He sent personal messages to Hitler and Mussolini appealing for a ten-year pledge not to attack or invade other countries. In late August of 1939, Russia and Germany signed a nonaggression pact. In spite of all of Father's efforts, Hitler invaded Poland and the die was cast. France and England honored their pledges to the government of Poland and declared war on Germany. The previous

January, Father had asked Congress for funds to expand our air force and to construct new naval air bases. In April of 1939, he warned our country of the approach of war in Europe. Many Americans urged the government to stay out of the conflict in Europe, but by September, Father deemed it necessary to urge Congress to repeal the embargo on the shipment of arms under the Neutrality Act, which he had signed reluctantly in 1937, at the time of the Spanish Civil War. Mother was becoming more and more alarmed at the thought that we might become involved in another world war. She had visions of all the young men who would be mobilized and sent into such a conflict.

As the year 1940 approached, it became evident that the world situation was deteriorating rapidly. To make matters worse, 1940 was a presidential election year, and decisions had to be made on how best to prepare our country for not only the crisis in Europe but also the growing threat of Japanese expansion in the Pacific. Mother watched the tension that was gripping her husband. His office hours were lengthening, and he had very little time to relax and unwind. She used to talk to him about finishing up the job of being president and what they would do after he retired. At first, he would animatedly discuss their plans for the future. He used to love to relate how he would retire to Hyde Park and they would both do a great deal of writing. In addition, he hoped that at least part of the year they would travel to all corners of the globe. At times, he even speculated on the chance that his successor as president would appoint him a roving ambassador to represent the country and negotiate with other governments on agreements vital to the interest of our nation.

As the seriousness of the conflict in Europe increased, he spoke less and less to her about his plans for future retirement. He was asking Congress for additional appropriations of over one billion dollars for defense. These moves were justified since Hitler was moving fast.

The retreat of the British army from Dunkirk was a sad and anxious time at the White House as well as for the people of Great Britain. Mother felt more and more that events were moving about the world in such a way that Father would never realize his ambition to retire at the end of his term. People came to her and said that there was nobody else who could lead the country in this time of international crisis. Mother asked Father on several occasions if he did not think he should make a definite effort to prepare someone to succeed him. Father answered that he thought people had to prepare themselves, that all he could do was to give them opportunities and see how they worked out.

As the time for the convention drew closer, it became evident that the Democratic party had not found anyone else that it thought could carry on in the office as president. It was a very sad moment for Mother when she realized that Father was being convinced by those around him that he should, and must, run for a third term. Everything in her being cried out with the desire for them to be able to retire from public life. It was with a heavy heart that she realized this was not to be. Finally, she was forced into going to the convention itself. She went out to Chicago after receiving a hurried call from Jim Farley. Upon her arrival, she found that things were in a pretty mess. It seems that Father had never told Jim Farley who his choice was for vice president. Jim Farley told her that he thought one of several candidates would be acceptable, mentioning that I was planning to second the nomination of Jesse Jones. As it turned out, Father wanted Henry Wallace to be his vice president, and Mother had to inform me just prior to my making the seconding speech that it would be in opposition to Father's choice. As a result, I made no nominating speech.

After she had straightened out the mix-up at the convention, she left immediately for Hyde Park. She was later to find out that a deep rift had developed because of Jim Farley's personal ambition, and that Father had not taken him into his confidence on the matter of his running mate. The truth of the matter is that Jim Farley had been convinced, almost up to the last minute, that Father would not run for a third term, and he hoped that the mantle would descend upon his shoulders and he would be selected as the standard-bearer of the Democratic party in that year. I think that Mother felt quite strongly that part of the confusion and animosity which developed prior to and after this campaign would have been avoided if Louis Howe had been alive and well at this period in Father's political history.

Wendell Willkie was nominated by the Republican party that summer. Father had a great deal of empathy for his opponent. He liked him very much and he never felt the same bitterness toward him that he felt toward some of his other opponents. Mother felt that Mr. Willkie was courageous and sincere, and she liked the way he stood for certain principles. Once the nomination was made, however, Mother wanted Father to win, mostly because she felt that that was what he wanted, and she would have been sorry, for his sake, if he had been defeated. She realized too that if he lost, he would go on living a good and full life, for he was a philosophical person who accepted and made the best of whatever happened. It is true that tradition was shattered when he won the election of 1940. No other president had won a third term. This meant that Mother had to bury her own desires and continue on as a public person, carrying out the duties of first lady as well as continuing her arduous schedule as her husband's right hand.

By this time, America was deeply divided over the question of our possible involvement in a war. The draft had been established about a year earlier, and many young people were bitter at the thought of being forced into military service. Others were violently opposed to our siding with Great Britain in her single-handed struggle against Hitler. Many popular and

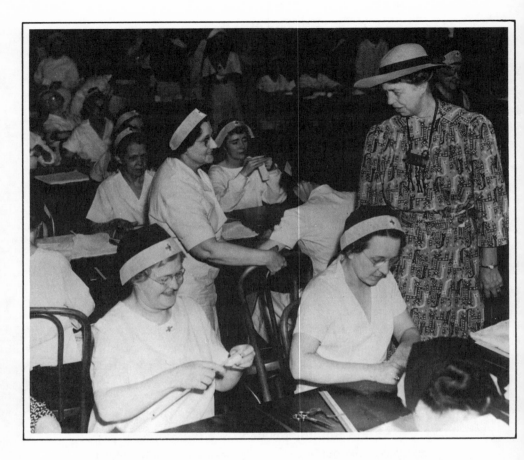

Mother inspects Red Cross volunteers in Washington, D.C., 1940.
UNITED PRESS INTERNATIONAL

respected Americans, such as Charles Lindbergh, professed admiration for Hitler and all he stood for. In spite of the difficulties of persuading the American people that we needed to be prepared, Father was able to continue the steady buildup of our armed forces.

His mobilizing of our industrial capacity for the military expansion enabled more and more people to find gainful employment on the factory assembly line. This period marked a revolution in our employment practices. Women were recruited to work on the assembly line and, before many years were to pass, women would become vital to the basic work force of our country. This marked the achieving of one of Mother's special goals: the emancipation of women. She took an enormous amount of satisfaction from the fact that when she went through a factory, she would see men and women performing the same tasks, and she used to delight in relaying the information back to Father that a certain foreman in such and such a plant had told her that the women workers were more efficient than the men workers. Watching this change in the acceptance of women in the work force had a profound effect on her outlook during the rest of her life.

❧ 11 ❧

Pearl Harbor

Following the sweeping electoral victory in 1940, the clouds of war continued to hang heavily upon the horizons, both in Europe and in Asia. Mother was much disturbed because three of her sons went on active duty in the armed services, I in 1940, and Franklin, Jr., and Jimmy in 1941. This portended to her the almost inevitable fact that our country would be drawn into the war. By the middle of 1941, millions of young American boys had been drafted into the service. Mother had a horror of what war would bring for the people of this country. She recognized that in World War I practically an entire generation of young men had been wiped out in England, France, and Germany. The United States' losses in World War I had been relatively light, but she recognized that if we had a second world war a great majority of the homes of America would lose loved ones in the conflict. Many events took place that made the mood in America even more tense.

Hitler invaded the Soviet Union and initially made huge inroads that the Soviet armies were hard-pressed to fend off. The president went on a mysterious trip which he could not reveal beforehand to Mother. It turned out to be a meeting with Winston Churchill at Argentia, Newfoundland. This was the first real opportunity that Mr. Churchill and Father had to get to know each other, and, as it turned out, to form a mutual liking for each other. One of the things that gave Father the most satisfaction about this trip was that he was able to pull it off without ever having the press discover anything about it.

In September of 1941, two deaths in quick succession saddened the hearts of Mother and Father. Father's mother, Sarah Delano Roosevelt, died on September 7. Father had always had a very close bond of love and affection with his mother, but Mother's feelings had been strained at times as a result of her mother-in-law's efforts to dominate and shape Mother's life. The very night that Granny died, Mother was called away to Vassar Hospital in Poughkeepsie, where her brother, Hall, had been taken after falling ill. Right after her mother-in-law's funeral, she moved Hall to Walter Reed Hospital in Washington, at his request. There she spent several weeks watching her brother grow weaker. On September 25 he died. Later my mother was to write, "The loss of a brother is always a sad breaking of a family tie, but in the case of my brother it was like losing a child. He had come to live with us when we were first married, and from then on Franklin and I had been his closest family."

After this loss, Mother threw herself into a job which she had accepted from Mayor La Guardia of New York City. This job entailed organizing the civilian defense of the city of New York. One morning Father said, "What's this I hear? You didn't get to bed at all last night?" She had been working on her mail without regard to time, and when it began to get light, she decided it was not worthwhile going to bed. She found in this job that even though she worked without salary or paid expenses, she became the target for fault-finding by members of the opposition.

Under Mayor Fiorello La Guardia (*right*), Mother worked as assistant director of the Office of Civilian Defense for New York City.
FRANKLIN D. ROOSEVELT LIBRARY

The fateful day of December 7, 1941, began in a quiet manner. A large party was expected for lunch, and Mother was disappointed but not surprised when Father sent word a short time before lunch that he did not see how he could join the group. He had been increasingly worried and frequently at the last moment would tell her that he could not come to some gathering or other that had been arranged. Sometimes Father decided to eat alone in his study; sometimes he had Harry Hopkins or a secretary eat with him, or a person with whom he wished to talk privately. Harry Hopkins ate with Father in the study that day, and there were thirty-one guests at Mother's lunch. By the time lunch was over, news had come of the attack on Pearl Harbor, but none of them heard it until they went upstairs, when one of the ushers told Mother. The information was so stunning that there was complete quiet, and the guests went off to carry out their afternoon tasks in a kind of vacuum. Mother saw the guests off and waited until Father was alone to slip into his study, but she realized he was concentrating on what had to be done and would not talk about what had happened until this first strain was over. So she went back to work. A few minutes after 3:00 P.M., the secretaries of war and navy, Admiral John Beardall—Father's naval aide—Secretaries McIntyre and Early, and Grace Tully were all in Father's study on the second floor of the White House. They were soon joined by General George C. Marshall and the secretary of state. Later, when Father did have a chance to talk, she thought that in spite of his anxiety he was, in a way, more serene than he had appeared in a long time. One could no longer do anything but face the fact that this country was in a war; from here on, difficult and dangerous as the future looked, it presented a clearer challenge than had the long uncertainty of the past.

The next day, Mother heard her husband as he addressed the combined houses of Congress. She was deeply unhappy as she listened to the president announcing our entry into World War II. It seemed to her that she was living again the day when President Wilson addressed the Congress to announce our entry into World War I. When we entered World War I, she worried about the safety of her husband and her brother. Now, as she listened to her husband, she knew that her sons would be committed to combat.

She did feel a sense of uplift as the days went by because of the unity expressed by the citizens of America. At all the enlistment points around the country, hundreds of thousands of young, middle-aged, and older men lined up to volunteer their services in the armed forces. Hundreds of thousands more older people, housewives, and young girls lined up outside the factories manufacturing our war materiel to apply for jobs on the assembly line. At this one time in its history, our country was unified in single-minded purpose as it had never been before and as, possibly, it will never be again.

From Pearl Harbor Day on, Mother redoubled her efforts to keep a steady stream of letters and communications going back and forth with her sons in the service. She lived in constant dread of hearing that a fatal accident had befallen one of the boys in combat. She savored every letter that she received from them, and she kept in constant touch with their families. She would bring, on numerous occasions, one daughter-in-law or another together with the grandchildren to the White House or to Hyde Park, so that she could pass on to the absent sons details of their families.

Her day-to-day White House responsibilities became ever more taxing. Almost immediately after Pearl Harbor, Winston Churchill decided that he had to come in person to present the cause of the British empire and to impress upon the president that the United States had to keep supplying Great Britain with the sinews of war. At the same time, the Russian ambassador was importuning the president on the desperate plight of the Soviet Union in trying to repel the invading German forces. Both supplicants cried out for bigger and bigger shipments of American arms with which to repel the attacker.

❧ *12* ❧

In Wartime England

In the fall of 1942, Mother had an invitation from Queen Elizabeth to go to Great Britain to see the work the women were doing in the war and to visit our servicemen stationed there. What she did not realize was that Father was anxious and eager for her to go over to England so that he could get a firsthand report from her about our servicemen who were stationed in England. He knew that those same men would shortly be embarking for the North African invasion. Her visit to England proved to be a high point in my own personal military career.

On this visit, the queen requested that Mother stay at Buckingham Palace.

As Mother neared London, she grew more and more nervous about her visit and wondered why she had ever let herself be inveigled into coming on this trip. Finally, they pulled into the station. The red carpet was unrolled, and the stationmaster and the head guard on the train, both of them looking grand enough to be high officials of the government, told Mother that the moment to get off had arrived. There stood King George and Queen Elizabeth and many high military officials of both nations.

After the formal greeting, the king and queen took Mother to their car, while Malvina Thompson, who had accompanied her, was taken in hand by the lady-in-waiting and two gentlemen from the royal household, and the whole group drove off to Buckingham Palace.

The king and queen treated her with the greatest kindness. The feeling that she had had about them during their visit to the United States—that they were simply a young and charming couple who would have to undergo some very difficult experiences—began to come back to her, intensified by the realization that they now had been through these experiences and were anxious to tell her about them. In all her contacts with them, she gained the greatest respect for both the king and queen. She did not always agree with the ideas expressed to her by the king on international subjects, but the fact that both of them were doing an extraordinarily outstanding job for their people, in the most trying times, impressed her.

When they arrived at the palace, she was taken to her rooms. It was explained to her that she could have only a small fire in her sitting room and one in the outer waiting room, and they hoped she would not be too cold. They pointed out the shell holes through the windows. The window panes in her room had all been broken and replaced by wood and isinglass and one or two small panes of glass. Later, the queen showed her where a bomb had dropped right through the king's rooms, destroying both his room and hers. They explained the various layers of curtains which had to be kept closed when the lights were on, and informed her that there would be a messenger outside the door to take her to the drawing room at the proper hour for dinner.

Buckingham Palace seemed perfectly enormous to Mother. The suite she had was so huge that when I saw it, I told Mother she would have to take the long corridor at the White House for her bedroom, because the one she had would never again seem adequate. The wardrobes were wonderful, the kind one longs for at home, but the fifty-five-pound limit on baggage made her few clothes look pathetic hanging in those wardrobes. Mother wondered what the maid thought when she unpacked them. One evening dress, two daytime dresses, one suit and a few blouses, one pair of walking shoes, and one pair of evening shoes comprised her whole wardrobe for a visit to Buckingham Palace! One of the newspaper women, for want of something better to write about, later reported that Mother had worn the soles of her only pair of shoes through. The head usher at the White House read the story and thoughtfully sent her another pair.

After Mother's arrival, the king and queen took her to look at the devastation of London. Blocks upon blocks were reduced to rubble. The German Luftwaffe had brought about great destruction within the city and in other areas in England, but Mother remarked on the extraordinary determination and strength which the rank and file of the British people exhibited.

On this her first visit overseas to a combat area, Mother started a practice which she continued on subsequent trips wherever she visited our troops. As she met the boys and talked to them, she would get the names and addresses of their families so that she could write to them on her return to the United States. Many thousands of families received such letters from Mother throughout the country.

On the occasion of another dinner with Prime Minister and Mrs. Winston Churchill, Mother inadvertently had a difference of opinion with Prime Minister Churchill on the subject of loyalist Spain. The prime minister had asked whether we, the United States, were sending "enough" to Spain and whether it was reaching there safely. Henry Morgenthau, who was present at the dinner, said that he hoped we were, but Mother said that she thought it was a little too late, that we should have done something to help the loyalists during the Civil War. Mr. Churchill said that he had been for the Franco government until Germany and Italy went into Spain to help Franco. Mother remarked that she could not see why the loyalist government could not have been helped, and the prime minister's reply was that he and Mother would have been the first to lose their heads if the loyalists had won.

My experience with Mother's visit to England had its amusing moments. At that time, I was commanding a photo reconnaissance group that was being trained to go in on the invasion of North Africa. We were stationed at an airfield near the village of Steeple Morden. Mother was driving out from London in an embassy car for her visit to my outfit. There were no signs permitted on the highways because of the threat of a German invasion. Understandably, the embassy driver become lost. After a couple of hours of futile attempts to find the way, a call was placed back to our London embassy. Mother's code name for her travels in England was Rover. The embassy man calling for directions to his embassy reported, "Rover has lost her pup." Finally, directions were given and Mother found her way to our air station. My one thousand troops had been lined up for four hours in a driving rain to receive her. When she arrived and saw the sodden boys all lined up at attention, she quickly asked that they be dismissed and allowed to return to quarters to change into dry clothes. A great cheer went up at this request. Although this was the only time that I was to see Mother while stationed overseas, it did prepare me for the thrill of meeting Father in North Africa at Casablanca, and somewhat later when he reviewed my troops which had grown into an international allied wing, with three thousand men. This time the sun shone as the president drove past in a jeep, inspecting the allied squadrons.

During her visit to England in the fall of 1942, Mother reviews my troops at the U.S. Army Air Force base.   UNITED PRESS INTERNATIONAL

I can attest to the great boost it gave to our troops in Great Britain to have Mother visiting with them. I also know, first-hand, of the delight and affection with which the British people greeted her as she traveled throughout that war-torn country. Her unaffected interest and concern for all those she met on that trip was truly inspiring to me, and it gave me a pride in the leadership of our country.

❧ *13* ❧

Boosting Morale
in the Pacific

On January 9, 1943, Father took off alone, leaving Mother behind, on his first long airplane trip. He journeyed out on the
first *Air Force One*, an Army Air Force C-54. He traveled down
to Brazil, across the south Atlantic, and north up the African
coast to Casablanca. When he returned from this trip, he had
many stories to tell Mother. One of his stories concerned his reactions to General Charles de Gaulle. He commented, in talking
to Mother, "General de Gaulle is a soldier, patriotic, yes, devoted to his country; but on the other hand he is a politician
and a fanatic, and there are, I think, in him almost the makings
of a dictator." Another thing that Father was disturbed about
was the horrible condition of the natives in the places where he
had stopped. Mother said that he reported to her that he had
never minced words in telling Mr. Churchill that he did not
think the British had done enough to improve the lot of the na-
tive people in any one of the colonial areas he had seen on this
trip. I must say that I covered a great deal of African territory
during my service in World War II, and I could not agree more
with him about his assessment. I would have gone further and

FAMILY KITCHEN.

ENTER
HERE

Madame Chiang Kai-shek visits Mount Vernon with Mother on Washington's birthday in 1943.   FRANKLIN D. ROOSEVELT LIBRARY

said that all of the colonies controlled by European nations suffered under the domination of their colonial masters.

Later, Mother had her first meeting with Madame Chiang, the wife of Generalissimo Chiang Kai-shek of China. Mother's assessment of her was quite interesting. I feel that I must quote Mother's own words in describing this historically important lady.

"I shall never forget the day I went with her when she addressed the House of Representatives, after meeting the senators. A little slim figure in Chinese dress, she made a dramatic entrance as she walked down the aisle, surrounded by tall men.

She knew it, for she had a keen sense of the dramatic. Her speech, beautifully delivered, was a remarkable expression of her own conception of democracy. I saw another side of Madame Chiang while she was in the White House, and I was much amused by the reactions of the men with whom she talked. They found her charming, intelligent, and fascinating, but they were all a little afraid of her, because she could be a cool-headed statesman when she was fighting for something she deemed necessary to China and to her husband's regime; the little velvet hand and the low, gentle voice disguised a determination that could be as hard as steel.

"A certain casualness about cruelty emerged sometimes in her conversations with the men, though never with me. I had painted for Franklin such a sweet, gentle and pathetic figure that, as he came to recognize the other side of the lady, it gave him keen pleasure to tease me about my lack of perception."

The year 1943 found Mother making her second overseas trip. Father said he thought it would be a good idea for Mother to visit our servicemen scattered throughout the Pacific area, and at the same time she could pay a visit to New Zealand and Australia. She had received a number of letters from women in those two countries who suggested that since Mother had seen the work being done by the women of Great Britain she really ought to come and see what women were doing on the opposite side of the world. She embarked on this long journey, having agreed at the request of Mr. Norman Davis, Chairman of the American Red Cross, to inspect the Red Cross installations in the Pacific area. She also agreed to wear a Red Cross uniform throughout her trip. A great many derogatory columns were written in the American press regarding this trip because of the fact that she traveled on military aircraft and stayed in military installations. This mode of travel seemed to irk the opposition in our country. Actually, she was so anxious to follow the correct protocol that she and Father both decided that she should not keep any of the money that accrued from

During World War II, Mother traveled to the Pacific to visit U.S. military stationed there. Here she talks with servicemen at the Red Cross canteen in Cairns, Australia.   FRANKLIN D. ROOSEVELT LIBRARY

her column while she was on this trip. She arranged for half of her earnings to go to the Red Cross and for the other half to go to the American Friends Service Committee, also dividing between them what she earned from articles written after her return.

There were many wonderful stories that Mother recounted about this trip. One of the first described her visit to Christmas Island. There she had her first encounter with tropical bugs. When she walked into her room late one night and turned on the light, she found the floor completely covered with little red bugs. She recounted that she nearly disgraced herself by screaming, but realized that being the only woman on the island her screams would undoubtedly cause a tremendous furor. Instead, she stamped her foot, and all the bugs disappeared through the cracks in the floor. She remembered the advice of her sons: "Don't eat all your meals with the brass." As a result, she would get up every morning at 6:00 in order to have breakfast with the enlisted men. Her visit with Admiral William F. Halsey, at Noumea, was fraught with tension. Admiral Halsey, when he learned of her visit to the South Pacific, had expressed grave reservations. The admiral dreaded his first meeting with Mother but not any more than she dreaded her meeting with him. But evidently she made a very good impression on the admiral, because he arranged for her to visit the soldiers on Guadalcanal and other parts of the Pacific fighting areas. Mother told one story about a visit to a Red Cross club. There she heard about a boy in the club who said he did not want to speak to or even be in the same room with Mother because he understood that she advocated that all the marines who came to the Pacific should be quarantined for six months after their return. Whether this story had started as a propaganda broadcast by Tokyo Rose, or whether it was a story spread by the hate-Roosevelt contingent in the U.S., no one seemed to know, but it had been spread far and wide through the ranks of the marine divisions.

Mother wrote in detail of her visit to Guadalcanal. They arrived at 6:00 A.M., and they had breakfast with the commanding officer on the airfield; he was a great friend of Admiral Halsey. Then the army officers came to get Mother, and, as they drove off, the trucks with the men who were working on the field were just arriving. Colette Ryan, a friend of Admiral Halsey, and Mother leaned out to wave. At first, there was complete surprise on the faces of the men, and then one boy in stentorian tones said, "Gosh, there's Eleanor." Mother's reaction was ambivalent. She didn't know whether they were glad to see her, or whether they were derisive, but they were so evidently pleased to see women, she had to laugh and to keep on waving. The commanding officer was plainly horrified to have her treated with such levity, so she tried to make believe she considered it a great compliment. She visited all the improvements that had been made since this part of the island came into our possession. There were thought to be some Japanese still on the other side of the island and there were still air raids.

After her visit to Guadalcanal, she flew back by way of Christmas Island because an attack was being made by the Japanese on the route that had been originally planned. Upon her arrival in Hawaii, she spent several days before returning to California. On this journey, she covered a fantastic amount of territory. She had been to Hawaii, Christmas Island, Penryhn Island, Bora Bora, Aitutaki, Tutuila, Samoa, Fiji, and New Caledonia; Auckland, Wellington, and Rotorua in New Zealand; Sydney, Canberra, Melbourne, Rockhampton, Cairns, and Brisbane in Australia; Efate, Espíritu Santo, Guadalcanal, and Wallis. The trip had not been without a tremendous physical toll. She lost thirty pounds and admitted to being more tired than she had ever been in her entire life.

She gained lasting impressions from her two overseas visits. She expressed her vivid reluctance at visiting the hospitals where the wounded were being cared for. First there was the physical fatigue of walking through miles of hospital wards day after day, but far worse for her was the terrible realization of the waste and the resentment that burned within her as she wondered why men could not sit down around a table and settle their differences before an infinite number of the youth of many nations had to suffer. She commented later that the most horrifying hospitals were those in which the men who had been mentally affected by the experiences that they had been through were treated. She felt that these men would probably have broken under other circumstances and that there must be something wrong with our civilization when our young people were so vulnerable to mental illness. Her horror at seeing people who had broken mentally and emotionally made her lie awake nights.

In the latter part of the year, Father left on his second overseas journey. On this trip, he went to Cairo for his meeting with Generalissimo and Madame Chiang Kai-shek and Winston Churchill. Afterward, he and Mr. Churchill flew to Teheran where they had their first summit meeting with Marshal Stalin. The end of that year found Mother and Father reunited in the White House, both having a sense of exhilaration and achievement. They felt that a turning point had been reached, and that victory over the Germans and the Japanese was now only a matter of time.

🐚 14 🐚

Tragedy

The year 1944 was to turn into an especially strenuous one. In March, Mother took off on her third big wartime trip. She was to travel over 13,000 miles by plane, through parts of the Caribbean and Latin America. Father had insisted that she take this trip. While the threat of war had receded in the area, we had many military men stationed at strategic points to guard our shipping lanes. These men felt that they were in a backwater and that they had been stuck away from the more important war areas. Father reasoned that a visit from Mother would help the men realize how their government recognized that they were doing a vital job and that they had not been forgotten, even though they might not be on the front line. She had an opportunity to look up many GI's whose families had contacted her asking for information about their loved ones if she ever ran across them, and she was able to bring messages back from thousands of lonesome men longing for the day when they could return home. June 6, 1944, was a red-letter day. The invasion of the continent of Europe from England was accomplished on that day, and Father went on the air to deliver his

Mother visits the enlisted men's club on the Galápagos Islands, off the coast of Ecuador, during her trip to Central and South America, 1944.   FRANKLIN D. ROOSEVELT LIBRARY

now famous D-Day Prayer. Everyone in the country seemed to be holding his or her breath, waiting for news as to whether the invasion would prove successful. There was a great sense of relief in the White House as the news came in, little by little, confirming that the landings on the beaches had been completed, that permanent installations had been set up, and that the liberation of Europe had really begun. The invasion had taken a fairly heavy toll of casualties, and Mother's heart went out to the many families who would be receiving news of the death or wounding of their cherished ones over the next few days.

Another presidential election was coming in November, and Mother realized that there was no question that Father would insist on running for the presidency for a fourth time. He was convinced that he should remain at the helm until total victory had been achieved. Mother had some reservations because she felt that the strain upon Father's health had been severe. During the winter, he had run a troublesome fever from which he was very slow in recovering. Father underwent a rigorous physical examination before making up his mind on running again. The doctors prescribed certain rules that he was to follow so that he could stand up to the strain of going on with his work.

In August of that year, Mother and Father were greatly saddened by the death of Marguerite "Missy" LeHand. She had lived with Mother and Father practically as a member of the family for many years. She had taken over so many times when Mother was away on trips, and Father had been dependent upon her never-failing attention to his needs. Mother had always been grateful to her for her loyalty and had come to regard her with enormous affection.

In September, Mother and Father went together to Quebec, Canada, to attend another war conference. The conference was necessarily brief because Father had to return to take up the campaign for the presidency. His first major speech of the campaign was made at the Teamsters union dinner in Washington. At this dinner, Father ridiculed the Thomas Dewey campaign by recounting the story of his little dog, Fala. He told how indignant Fala was over the Republican accusation that he, Fala, had been left behind on an island when Father was visiting the Aleutians and how he was retrieved only at the cost of untold sums of the taxpayers' money. Father ridiculed this silly charge by telling how it offended Fala's Scotch blood.

As the campaign came to a climax, Father and Mother had to drive through miles and miles of New York City streets in an open car in one of the worst rainstorms to hit that area in many a long year. Father was drenched through to the skin and caught a bad cold, from which he recovered slowly. The election was won rather handily, and Father and Mother went to Hyde Park for Christmas.

Early in January, they both realized that this would be his last inauguration, and over Mother's reluctant objection, Father insisted that all of their grandchildren should come to the White House for the inauguration on the twentieth. Most of the boys were overseas, and so it was that the mothers, with their thirteen offspring, all gathered at the White House for this last solemn occasion. It was clear, following the inauguration, that Father was not at all well, but he was determined that he would go to Yalta for a summit meeting with Churchill and Stalin. He also told Mother that he intended, if at all possible, to see some of the Arabs and to try to find a peaceful solution to the Palestine situation.

When he got back from his trip to Yalta and his visit with King Abdul ibn Saud of Saudi Arabia, he told Mother that the Yalta meeting had been only a step toward the ultimate solution of the problems of the postwar world. He knew that there would have to be many more negotiations and meetings in order to produce an era of peace and understanding.

Mother found that after Yalta, Father was less and less willing to see people for any length of time and that he needed to rest in the middle of the day. She was delighted when he decided to go to Warm Springs for a rest. He invited his cousins, Laura Delano and Margaret Suckley, to go with him.

On April 12, 1945, Mother received a call at the White House from Laura Delano. She learned that Father had fainted while sitting for his portrait and had been carried to bed. Father's physician at the White House, Dr. Ross McIntire, was not alarmed but he and Mother planned to go down to Warm Springs that evening. She proceeded with her afternoon engagements. She was at a benefit at the Sulgrave Club in Washington when she was called to the telephone. Father's press secretary, Steve Early, was on the phone, very much upset. He asked her to come home at once. All the way back to the White House, she knew in her heart what had happened. Steve Early and Dr. McIntire broke the news. Word had come through from Dr. Howard Bruenn in Warm Springs, first of the hemorrhage, and later of Father's death. Mother immediately sent for Vice President Truman and made arrangements to leave for Warm Springs by plane that evening.

When the vice president came, she could think of nothing to say except that how sorry she was for him, and how she wanted to offer any aid that she could to help him. She then prepared a cable to be sent to all four of us boys: "FATHER SLEPT AWAY. HE WOULD EXPECT YOU TO CARRY ON AND FINISH YOUR JOBS."

She then went out to the airplane and flew down to Warm Springs. Upon her arriving, she found that "they were all stunned and sad but everyone was as self-controlled and calm as possible. Though this was a terrible blow, somehow one had no chance to think of it as a personal sorrow. It was the sorrow of all those to whom this man, who now lay dead, and who happened to be my husband, had been a symbol of strength and fortitude."

Mother took charge as the body was moved to the railroad station where it was placed on a special train for the return to Washington. Mother described the trip as follows: "I lay in my berth with the window shade up, looking out at the countryside he had loved and watching the faces of the people at stations, and even at the crossroads, who came to pay their last tribute all through the night."

In Washington, the coffin was taken by caisson from the railroad station to the White House. It was placed in the East Room. It was briefly opened so that Mother could go in alone to put a few flowers in before she finally had it closed. Both she and Father had always had an aversion to the custom of having a person lie in state with an open coffin so that crowds could file by for a last view of the deceased. Both of them felt that they would prefer to be remembered as they were when they were alive.

One incident occurred concerning Mother's decision to have the coffin closed to public view. The Soviet ambassador requested that he and his deputies be permitted to view the body. Mother demurred but they returned saying that Marshal Stalin had made the request. She refused again, and finally they came back a third time to tell her that Marshal Stalin considered it most important that he satisfy himself that Father had not been poisoned, as he was convinced there was a conspiracy to murder Father and himself. Later, I was to learn in an interview with Stalin that he believed Churchill was behind the conspiracy.

The funeral was to take place in Hyde Park. Only two of the children were able to attend the funeral. I returned from Europe. Jimmy tried desperately to get back in time, but he could not make it back until just after the funeral. Both Franklin, Jr., and John were at Okinawa, with no opportunity of returning to the States. Anna was already living at the White House, having moved in a year earlier to help Father.

I received my message from Mother on the evening of April 12. My commanding general, James Doolittle, and his superiors, General Carl Spaatz and General Dwight D. Eisenhower, all combined their efforts to secure passage for me on an aircraft returning to the United States. It just so happened that Father's good friend, Bernard Baruch, and his friend and speech writer, Samuel Rosenman, had been in London representing Father in negotiations with Churchill and members of his staff. They had an Air Force C-54 standing at an airport just north of London. They were preparing immediately to return to Washington in order to attend the funeral. I was ordered to return on that plane. I bade a hasty farewell to the members of my personal staff, and at 5:00 the next morning flew my own plane over to the airport where Sam Rosenman and Bernie Baruch were ready to take off. It was a sad flight, crossing the Atlantic in the company of Father's two old friends. But I must say that it was made easier for me during those long hours. Sam and Bernie kept up a lively conversation, in which they insisted that I participate. We talked a great deal, speculating on how long it would take—one week, two weeks, or even up to a month—to finally bring about the complete downfall of the Third Reich. They talked about the months ahead and what had to be done to bring about a hasty conclusion to the war against the Japanese. Never did they refer to the enormous loss that they felt about Father's passing. They didn't want me to dwell on the subject. They were very, very kind.

❧ 15 ❧

Picking Up the Pieces

After the funeral ceremony in the White House, the presidential train moved out of Washington carrying Father on his last ride to Hyde Park. All night long, Mother, Anna, and I watched out of the windows of the train. Large groups of people were standing along the railroad tracks the entire distance between Washington and Hyde Park. They had come to pay their last respects and to express their sorrow at the passing of the man who had been their president for over twelve years. As the train drew into the little station, practically every living soul who lived in the community of Hyde Park and thousands of others were gathered. The body was moved from the train and placed again on a caisson for the two-mile trip from the station to Father's boyhood home. All along the route, going south from the village at Hyde Park, the road was lined with silent mourners.

When we arrived at our family home, we turned down the driveway and followed the casket to the rose garden where Father had directed that he wanted to be buried. He had given detailed instructions as to the massive marble stone that was to mark the grave site. On the stone had been chiseled Mother's and Father's names. After Mother's name, the date of her birth had been carved, with a blank space following. After Father's name appeared the date of his birth, January 30, 1882, and the date of his death, April 12, 1945. The freshly dug grave was ready to receive Father's remains. The Reverend Gordon Kidd, of St. James Espiscopal Church in Hyde Park, conducted the funeral service. Family members stood to the right of the grave site, while President Truman and the other governmental and military leaders of our country were on the left. The service was conducted with great simplicity, and a squad of West Point cadets fired a last twenty-one-gun salute. With the bugler sounding taps, the body was slowly lowered into the earth. I glanced in the direction of my mother. Up to that time, the lines of her face had reflected the strain and emotion that she had been holding back over the last few days, but now, as the body was lowered and the clear notes of the bugle sounded in the still air, her face appeared calm and peaceful. The lines that had been deeply etched in her cheeks smoothed out, and her complexion looked almost like a young girl's. She stared straight ahead as she looked upon the marble marker that clearly said that someday she would be lying beside her husband.

It was probably the most memorable moment of my life. I realized more clearly than ever before the dedication to service of their fellowman that these two, my parents, had pledged to each other. There was much more to be done by my mother in the next few years, and it was quite clear that she was determined to carry on toward their joint goals.

After the burial, everyone walked the short distance to our big home. There, Mother received the mourners and thanked them all for coming to the ceremony. A couple of hours later, she departed with President and Mrs. Truman to take the same train back to Washington. She was determined immediately to start packing up all the personal possessions that had accumulated in twelve years of living at the White House. President and Mrs. Truman asked her please to take her time, but she acted with almost desperate urgency. She wanted to get away from the White House and she wanted to start reorganizing her own life. She wanted to put everything in order so that she could face the world and meet whatever challenges lay ahead.

In five days Mother moved out of the White House and into the apartment that she had had for several years on Washington Square in New York. For the rest of her life, she was to spend most of her time at home between her residence in New York and her cottage at Hyde Park.

The first task that faced Mother after leaving the White House was to figure out what was to become of the big old home at Hyde Park. In his will, Father had left the house, together with a substantial amount of surrounding acreage, to the federal government, but he had stipulated that if Mother or any of the children had wanted to live there, they could do so during their lifetime. Mother had already firmly made up her mind that never again did she want to run an elaborate household, but she asked each of her five children whether they had any desire to live in the old home. All five really would have liked the idea of living there, but not one of us could possibly have afforded to keep it up. The house itself could never have been run with fewer than four or five servants in the house, and the grounds, stables, and woods would have required an outside staff of at least four or five.

Arrangements were made to turn the main house and the grounds over to the federal government. Mother ensconced herself at her Val-Kill cottage, which was the refurbished factory that had been closed down a number of years before, two miles to the east, and there she made her permanent, comfortable home. As she turned her back on her old life, she had some personal thoughts.

"One cannot live the life Franklin led in Washington and keep up many personal friendships. A man in high public office is neither husband nor father nor friend in the commonly accepted sense of the words; but I have come to believe that Franklin stands in the memory of people as a man who lived with a great sense of history and with a sense of his obligation to fulfill his part as he saw it.

"On the whole, I think I lived those years very impersonally. It was almost as though I had erected someone outside myself who was the president's wife. I was lost somewhere deep down inside myself. That is the way I felt and worked until I left the White House.

"One cannot say goodbye to people with whom one has lived and who have served one well without deep emotion, but at last, even that was over. I was now on my own."

On Her Own

In 1958, four years before her death, Mother published another of her many books. This one was entitled *On My Own*. At the outset of this book, she recounted some of the changes that affected her life now that she was facing the world by herself. She wrote, "In the years immediately after Franklin's death, I discovered that financial matters could be rather nightmarish, because I was not a trained businesswoman. . . . But from the day of my husband's death it was clear that I would have to meet all the daily expenses of the apartment in New York, and, for a short time, of the big place at Hyde Park, which had a considerable payroll. Luckily, my husband had left me two life insurance policies. I used their proceeds while awaiting settlement of the estate, which amounted to approximately one million dollars. Then I had to make another decision. I could live on what my husband had left me and stop working. Or I could continue to work and to pay most of what I earned to the government in taxes. I don't suppose that there was much of a decision to make because, of course, I wanted to go on working. . . . I found in time that I could live on what I earned by writing, appearing on radio or television, and reading manuscripts at $100 per month for the Junior Literary Guild."

Her life became quite simple at the personal level. She later moved from her small apartment in New York to a four-story brownstone house in which she occupied the lower two floors, and her friend and doctor, Dr. David Gurewitsch, occupied the upper two floors. While she entertained constantly when in residence, she never had more than a couple to assist her at the Val-Kill cottage and a maid who came in at the New York residence. She accomplished a great deal of the grocery shopping herself and, for most of her life, drove her own car back and forth between Hyde Park and New York City. In New York, she was constantly taking taxicabs. The drivers invariably recognized her and struck up lengthy conversations. Many are the taxicab drivers who have recognized me when I have been in New York City and who have told me of the times that they had Mother in their taxicab and how much they loved her.

Mother's lecture schedule grew to about 150 engagements per year, and she started making numerous trips to all corners of the world. Very soon her average distance covered per year mounted to over half a million miles. Mother always said that she loved traveling because it gave her an opportunity to catch up on her reading. She remarked that she didn't grow weary of travel and that she did not tire easily, but she did complain quite frequently that her feet hurt. She used to say that she had White House feet. The doctors told her that her feet hurt largely because of a slight change in the bones of the instep that was caused by years of standing at receptions at the White House. Probably the only real complaint that Mother ever uttered about the hectic life that she lived was that she simply could not find time to read as much as she liked. Over the years, her reading habits had enabled her to be one of the best-read people in the world.

Mother's habit of having a constant stream of guests when at

[*107*]

home at Hyde Park led her mother-in-law to once remark that Mother liked to "keep a hotel." In the years that she lived at Val-Kill, there were plenty of guests ranging from the emperor of Ethiopia to her newest great-grandchild. She remarked that there were so many guests that they often arrived by the bus-load—perhaps a group of college students from various foreign countries or seventy-five or so employees of the United Nations who came for a picnic. Each year she had a picnic for 150 youngsters from the Wiltwyck School for Boys. She related that one day when there were eight staying at the cottage, a man with whom she had some business telephoned about mid-morning and said he would like to drop by. Then he added that he would like to bring his wife and daughter, too. A few minutes later a neighbor called to say he would like to bring over a friend—and the friend's two children. There were other calls and, finally, there were eighteen for luncheon. Eating out-doors—whenever the weather permitted—on the porch or picnic ground was the rule, and the food was always simple. Mother never cooked if she could help it, but any cook she had must be expert at whipping up a soufflé or scrambled eggs or other dishes that could be prepared quickly and eaten quickly. So, as was usually the case, she got by.

Mother's visits from dignitaries around the world were occasioned by her being the widow of the president of the United States, but, more importantly, by the fact that she served as an ambassador from the United States to the United Nations. She was appointed to this post by President Truman, and she went to London in January 1946, as a member of the U.S. delegation to the first regular constituted meeting of the United Nations. She was elected as the chairman of the Human Rights Commission of that body.

During the period that Mother was a member of the United Nations, as a U.S. delegate, she developed many of the personal attributes that distinguished her from most of her other fellow delegates. She became an able team player. She developed the

Talking with Haile Selassie, emperor of Ethiopia, during his visit to
Hyde Park   FRANKLIN D. ROOSEVELT LIBRARY

As head of the United Nations Commission on Human Rights, Mother was instrumental in formulating a Universal Declaration of Human Rights. Here she opens the seventeenth session in Geneva, Switzerland. UNITED NATIONS

ability to stifle her own strong views, and to work with other members of the U.S. delegation, such as Senators Arthur Vandenburg and Tom Connolly. Another member of the delegation, Mr. John Dulles, once remarked to Senator Vandenburg that Mrs. Roosevelt was certainly a most cooperative member of the delegation. For seven years, she served as a delegate. She was given universal credit for hammering out the agreement on the wording for the Declaration of Human Rights, which was adopted by the United Nations. This document has served as a beacon of hope for the people of most of the nations of the world. The Helsinki Accords was an extension of this docu-

With Senator Arthur Vandenburg (*left*) and Senator Warren Austin, Mother served as a U.S. delegate to the United Nations. They are attending the third session of the UN General Assembly in 1949.   UNITED NATIONS

ment, as it was a keystone in the foreign policy of President Jimmy Carter's administration. Every president of the United States since the passage of the Declaration of Human Rights has included as a key part of American foreign policy a support of human rights.

Mother never failed to attend the regular meetings of the General Assembly. She was a familiar sight at these meetings, as she sat in her accustomed chair, usually listening intently to the debates and knitting away on a pair of socks or a sweater for the next Christmas gift to a member of the family. In between sessions, she traveled extensively throughout the world, mostly at the behest of some fellow delegate from another country.

During her service as an American representative to the United Nations, she strove to augment the humanitarian work that was being accomplished by different organizations within the United Nations. She recognized all too well that while the United Nations could accomplish a great deal in assisting undeveloped nations, there was no machinery in place whereby the United Nations could become an enforcer of peace around the world. She would dearly have loved to have forced all the nations to deposit all their major armaments in the hands of the United Nations, but she was frustrated in this desire because the members of our own delegation were against any such move. Official U.S. policy was that our nation must remain the strongest nation.

As I have stated, Emperor Haile Selassie of Ethiopia made an official visit to Mother at Hyde Park. During his visit, he sat down with Mother in front of the television set to watch a film of himself on the screen. He was fascinated, and Mother got worried that he wasn't going to have time for his rest period. This rest period had been strongly emphasized as necessary when Mother was being briefed regarding his visit. She turned to him and said, "Your Majesty, I believe you want to rest for half an hour alone." He did not turn his gaze from the television screen, but his reply was prompt. "Oh no, it is not necessary for me to be alone. I only wanted to take off my shoes for a little while." Still watching the screen, he pointed downward and added, "and my shoes are off." The emperor's shoes certainly were off, and he was wiggling his toes appreciatively. To show his pleasure for the informal visit, the emperor sent Mother four hundred pounds of Ethiopian coffee beans when he returned to his own country.

Another person who fascinated Mother when he came to visit at Hyde Park was Prime Minister Jawaharlal Nehru of India. His striking figure and his physical and moral courage impressed her greatly. She noted his remarkable intellectual abilities and the ease with which he could completely detach himself from his surroundings. She observed, "This power of self-detachment and concentration is less unusual in India, but it was something I had previously observed only in persons who had been a long time in solitary confinement. Mr. Nehru has the point of view of a man educated in the West, but at heart he is very much an Indian as well as very much a human being."

Of course, there were many other notables who visited Mother down through the years at her cottage at Hyde Park. The great and near great from all over the world dropped in to pay their respects. During the years immediately following World War II, I was privileged to live close by and to assist Mother in adapting herself to her new life. Those were fun years for me. I was able to help her in negotiating new contracts for her daily column with United Features Syndicate. I negotiated a new contract for her with *McCall's* magazine to replace her old contract with *Ladies' Home Journal.* I helped her in revising her agency agreements for her literary and lecture efforts. I was instrumental in organizing the syndication of a radio program, and produced for NBC a weekly television program. These projects were to form a large part of her earnings for the balance of her life and would enable her to carry on her extraordinary burden of public service and provide her with the funds to support her many charitable efforts.

One sidelight of Mother's first years at Val-Kill cottage was the presence of Father's pet Scottie dog, Fala. Mother always felt that Fala never really adjusted to Father's death. Mother loved to tell how Fala reacted: She would say that once, in 1945, when General Eisenhower came to lay a wreath on Father's grave, the gates of the regular driveway were open and his automobile approached the house accompanied by the wailing of the sirens of a police escort. "When Fala heard the sirens, his legs straightened out, his ears pricked up, and we knew that he

General Charles de Gaulle, president of France, pays an official visit to Hyde Park after Father's death.   UNITED PRESS INTERNATIONAL

General Dwight D. Eisenhower visits Father's grave at Hyde Park.
FRANKLIN D. ROOSEVELT LIBRARY

expected to see his master coming down the drive, as he had come so many times. Later, when we were living in the cottage, Fala always lay near the dining room door where he could watch both entrances just as he did when his master was there." Fala accepted Mother after Father's death, but he always gave the impression that she was just someone to put up with until the master returned. Many dogs eventually forget. Fala never really forgot. Whenever he heard sirens, he became alert and felt again that he was an important being, as he surely had felt when he was traveling with my father. Fala is buried now in the rose garden at Hyde Park.

❧ 17 ❧

Trips Abroad

As a young girl, Mother had gone to school in England. She had formed an early attachment for the British people and especially for the lovely countryside of the rural British Isles. Before the death of my father, she had visited England during the height of the war. After his death, she received an invitation to visit England for the unveiling of a statue of her husband. This statue is located in Grosvenor Square in London, close by the U.S. embassy. On this visit, she was invited for a weekend at Windsor Castle. Mother found that her hosts, King George VI and Queen Elizabeth, were as genuine and unaffected as usual. She was tremendously impressed with the easy manner of the king and his queen in keeping their family life on such a warm and friendly level. She was most amused when Princess Margaret was entertaining some young people and they had the phonograph turned up quite loudly, playing some of the latest popular records. When the king came into the room, he instantly asked, "Meg, the music is too loud. Will you please turn it down?"

On the occasion of this visit, the queen mother, Mary, was staying at the castle, and Mother noted the close similarity in words and actions between Queen Mary and her own mother-in-law. She was particularly amused to note that Queen Mary had the same tendency to try to dominate the family life of her son and his whole family.

Mother was struck by the serious mien of the young Princess Elizabeth, who was the heir to the throne. She found that Elizabeth was taking a great deal of interest in what was being done to solve the social problems of her country and, indeed, how the government was meeting its responsibilities for the people of England. Later, when Elizabeth became queen, Mother noted that her liveliness had not changed, but she still was very serious, understandably so, under the burden of her duties.

The design of the statue that was erected in Grosvenor Square had caused a heated argument. Sir Campbell Stuart, head of the Pilgrim Association, which raised the money for the memorial, and the sculptor Sir William Reid Dick, both felt strongly that Father should be depicted standing, facing into the wind. Winston Churchill, on the other hand, who was an artist himself, took issue. He argued that because Father could not walk, the statue should show him in a sitting position. Mother's reaction to all this was very much on her mind during the unveiling ceremony. After King George had spoken and then walked with her to the statue for the unveiling, she pulled a cord and, as the covering dropped away, she saw the statue showing Father as he was some years before his death. The figure was standing, with one hand gripping a cane and with the familiar cape flowing back from his shoulders. She thought that the statue gave the impression Father would have liked to leave with the British people. She never regretted that it was done as a standing figure. There are two shallow pools on either side of it and around the pools are low marble seats where, as the landscape architect had explained, "people could come and sit and eat their lunches." Carved on the back of the seats are the four freedoms declarations. The architect said he felt Father had always liked to have the people close to him, "and here I have made this possible," he added. In the years since, he has been proven right. There are always people there, and one rarely sees the statue without at least one small homemade bouquet resting on the marble base.

Mother was to make many more trips to England after 1948, and always she was received with great affection by the British people and the royal family. I think that they felt that she and Father had been steadfast in their friendship and their assistance when England was experiencing the most difficult period in its history.

Mother also had a great fondness for France. During her younger years, she had visited Paris and much of the countryside. The fact that she spoke fluent French enabled her to move about and to converse with the people easily. On her visits she would be invited to the presidential palace to confer with the president, but invariably she attempted to keep her official duties to a minimum while she was in Paris. On several occasions when I was with her, I remember she would excitedly plan to try out a new restaurant that she had heard of. In all of her life, Mother showed very little interest in food. She regarded meals as being a necessary evil, to refuel the body with energy. No one ever accused her of being a gourmet, but when in Paris, all this changed. Suddenly she became excited about going to a little restaurant on the Left Bank where she would find a delectable new dish. As a rule, Mother would be quite frugal in her expenditures for a meal, but when in Paris, she would think nothing of making a reservation at one of the very expensive restaurants, and she would not even wince at the size of the check when it was presented.

I did notice that when we went to the Louvre museum, she took particular pleasure in finding her favorite old masterpieces located exactly in the same places that she remembered them from her youth. Her hotels might change between visits, but she had a few old favorites, like the Crillon, to which she returned time and again.

Another trip that remains vividly in my mind is the one made in 1950, when Mother invited me and two of my children, Chandler and Elliott, Jr. (Tony), to go with her for the dedication of another statue of my father. This memorial had been erected in Oslo, Norway. Our visit was marked by the enormous friendship displayed by the Norwegian people. The royal family and all the government officials gave us a rousing welcome. The unveiling of the statue was most impressive, standing as it did looking out over the harbor at Oslo. My children and I thoroughly enjoyed our outing on the fjord with the crown prince and his son. Mother seemed tireless in carrying out all of her official duties. We had planned on a grand tour of the Scandinavian countries. This was to be more in the nature of a private holiday, a chance for Mother to relax and see new sites in countries she had never visited before.

We went to Stockholm first and found that Sweden had no intention of our having a private holiday. Mother and I and the two children spent most of our time on official visits to the royal palace and government dignitaries. Only when we reached Finland did we really have an opportunity to escape officialdom. After spending a couple of days in Helsinki we flew north to the city of Rovaniemi. Here we stayed in a lovely inn overnight in a city well north of the Arctic Circle. My two youngsters experienced a new sensation—twenty-four hours of sunlight!

When we left Finland, we visited Copenhagen, Denmark, where we stayed at the U.S. embassy. After that we paid a brief visit to Brussels, Belgium, and then went to Holland. Here we were entertained by Queen Wilhelmina and her family, after which we had the opportunity of paying a visit to the town from which the first Roosevelt had immigrated to the new world. The next leg of our journey took us to Luxembourg, where we stayed with the ambassador to that country from America, Mrs. Perle Mesta. Here, we were entertained by the

In 1950, Mother and I (*top left*) took two of my children, Chandler (*in front of me*) and Tony (*to my left*), on a memorable tour of Scandinavia. Here we are with Crown Prince Olav and Princess Martha of Norway, their children, and U.S. Ambassador and Mrs. Charles Bay.
FRANKLIN D. ROOSEVELT LIBRARY

During a visit to India in 1952, Mother chats with Prime Minister Nehru and his daughter, Indira Gandhi, at the prime minister's house.   PRESS INFORMATION BUREAU, GOVERNMENT OF INDIA

grand duchess of Luxembourg, and we had the opportunity to visit the castle where my grandmother's family, the Delanos, had come from. When Mother and our little group arrived, we found that the old castle, which dated back many centuries, was still occupied by members of the Delano family. These were distant cousins of ours, probably going back twenty or more generations before we would have had a common ancestor.

Our holiday ended with brief visits to Paris and London and then back home. It was a memorable experience for me as well as for my two children.

❧ 18 ❧

Facing East:
in Japan and Hong Kong

One of the more interesting trips that Mother made was in 1953, when she went to Japan under the auspices of Columbia University. The reason that the Japanese wanted Mother to visit their country was that Japanese women were just coming into the responsibilities of functioning in a democracy after centuries of feudalism. As Mother remarked, "The attempt to change over to more or less democratic concepts in a short time naturally created many problems both of a political nature and in regard to family life. Some of the Japanese leaders hoped that an American woman talking to groups of Japanese women and men would be able to explain to them the meaning of democracy and the manner in which a democratic government functioned. The fact was, that after World War II, the United States had rather arbitrarily insisted on giving the Japanese a democratic constitution, telling them that now they were going to be a democratic country. But this, of course, did not automatically change the old customs or turn feudalism into democracy."

This was Mother's first visit to Japan and her first impression upon arrival was that the hotel accommodations were just as comfortable as they were back home. One feature that particu-

Mother is entertained at a tea ceremony in Kyoto, Japan.   FRANKLIN
D. ROOSEVELT LIBRARY

larly appealed to her was the sunken bathtub in her hotel room. She had not found that in any hotels before, and the ease of stepping down into one's bathtub rather than climbing in was a novelty for her. During her first press conference, she marveled at the hordes of newspaper photographers that attended her every move. They were to follow her throughout her entire visit.

As she went around the countryside, she noted that in the few short years since the conquering of Japan by the United States the people exhibited a great deal of friendship for her. This was spite of the fact that they deeply resented American troops in their homeland and were overly impressed with the military might of the United States.

In drafting the Japanese constitution, the basic document was prepared in English and translated into Japanese. Mother questioned whether the acceptance of that constitution by the Japanese people was really based on their understanding of it. She found that the exact meaning of the constitution was a burning question whenever she spoke to students or to members of the labor organizations.

Probably the most emotional experience that Mother encountered on her trip to Japan was her visit to Hiroshima. This is the place where the first atom bomb ever to be dropped on human beings was actually used. Mother's comments on this visit are worthy of our consideration today: "The people of the United States believe that our leaders thought long and carefully before they used this dreaded weapon. We know that they thought first of the welfare of our own people, that they believed the bomb might end the war quickly, with less loss of life everywhere, than if it had not been dropped. In spite of this conviction, one still cannot see a city and be shown the area that was destroyed by blast and fire and be told of the people who died or were injured, one cannot see the photographs of some of the victims, without a deep sadness. To see the home where orphans were being cared for was to wish with one's whole heart that man could learn from this, that we know too well how to destroy, and that we must learn, instead, how to prevent such destruction. . . . God grant to men greater wisdom in the future." The visit to Hiroshima convinced Mother of the futility of war, no matter how it might be justified.

The last part of Mother's visit was taken up with the usual visit to royalty. By the time that Mother made this trip to Japan she had met the royalty of many nations. Yet in spite of her past experiences she admitted to a twinge of anxiety as she prepared for her interview with the Emperor Hirohito and the Empress Nagako. During the five weeks that Mother spent in Japan, she had learned that the advisers around the emperor had in the past used his power to influence the people. The people themselves venerated the emperor almost as a god. But since Japan's defeat in World War II, Emperor Hirohito had disclaimed that he was a god, and he had traveled about the country meeting his people and seeing how things were going with his own eyes. Mother had felt, during her visit and talks with groups of women, that while women were a force in their homes behind the scenes, they had not gained direct equality with men as provided by their new constitution. Therefore, Mother requested that she have an opportunity to meet with the empress as well as the emperor.

On the way to the palace, the omnipresent Japanese photographers were waiting to snap pictures. Mother sat beside the empress on a sofa, and the emperor sat in an armchair across from Mother. Once they were seated, the emperor began the conversation and stated how he had always regretted that we had gone to war, in spite of his vigorous efforts to prevent it. Now, he said, he hoped we were embarked on an era of friendship and peace. Mother felt that he was sincere in saying that he had tried to prevent the war. Even at that time, he was hoping that Japan would become a member of the United Nations, as it later did, and that we could all work together for harmonious international relations.

During the interview, Mother disregarded the protocol that one should speak only when spoken to. She asked questions herself, especially addressed toward the empress in order to draw her out. She had heard that the empress was a woman of extensive education who had always taken a great interest in child education. Mother was curious about the empress and the severe discipline which was imposed upon her. For instance, the children of the imperial family each lived in a separate palace and visited their parents only a few times each week. Mother's remark when she heard this was, "What a strange family life!" She wondered aloud if maybe this stern discipline accounted for the look of calm that was on the face of the empress, but she also wondered if that calm could be attained without missing something in life.

Mother remarked to the empress on the many changes that were taking place throughout the world, particularly in the status and activities of women. The empress said nothing for a few moments after this observation and then replied, "We need more education." And then she continued, "There are great changes coming about in the life of our women. We have always been trained in the past to a life of service and I am afraid that as these new changes come about there may be a loss of real values. What is your impression, Mrs. Roosevelt?" Mother's answer was that in all eras of change there was a real danger that the old values would be lost. That would seem much less dangerous, "when the intelligent and broadminded women who have had an opportunity to become educated take the lead to bring about the necessary changes." At this point the emperor broke in, "Our customs are different, Mrs. Roosevelt. We have government bureaus to lead in our reforms. We serve as an example to our people in the way we live and it is our lives that have influence over them."

When Mother left Japan, she stopped in Hong Kong, where she had the opportunity of seeing how the free world and the communist world could live side by side. She found that there was a single strand of barbed wire separating the free territory of Hong Kong from China, and there was a bridge guarded by police over which a considerable number of Chinese went back and forth each day. These Chinese lived on the communist side but owned land on the Hong Kong side, and they were permitted to cross each morning to work the land. Then in the evening they returned across the bridge to the communist side. Mother was impressed at the small number of guards on either side of the border, even though large numbers of Chinese were continuing to flee across the frontier to Hong Kong every day or so.

One of the lovely personal stories that Mother told of her visit to Hong Kong concerned Government House. She met a Mr. Keswick, a British merchant, whose family had been in China for a very long time. She told Mr. Keswick that her husband's family had been in the China trade, and it turned out that he knew all about Russell & Company, in which the partners were Father's grandfather, Warren Delano, and his son-in-law, Will Forbes, and another son-in-law, Frederic Delano Hitch. She turned to Mr. Keswick and said, "There is one thing that you may be able to clear up for me. At home during the New Deal era, certain newspaper writers, who were opposed to the administration, often liked to assert that Franklin's family had made money in the opium trade in the days when the clipper ships sailed to China. I never knew whether such statements were true, so I never made any attempt to refute them. But perhaps you know." Mr. Keswick replied that it was true that all foreign merchants trading in tea in China in those days were required to obtain special permits. One of the requirements for getting a permit was that they agreed to carry a small amount of opium when they were purchasing tea or other goods to take to foreign lands. So Mother finally came to the conclusion that the cargoes did contain opium, no matter how limited.

❧ 19 ❧

Communism Firsthand:
in Yugoslavia and the Soviet Union

After Mother left Japan and went to Hong Kong, she stopped briefly in Turkey and Greece. In Greece she paid a formal visit to King Paul and Queen Frederika. Her comments about this king and queen mostly were confined to remarks about their informality, such as their driving sports cars at high speeds through the countryside. She felt that the king was rather unbending, but she found that the queen exhibited great warmth and intelligence. She was most disheartened with the enormous poverty that she saw, and she remarked on the number of orphans in the country, which had been devastated by so much war and disaster.

Following her rather brief visit in Greece, she next had the opportunity of going to Yugoslavia. She was interested in meeting with Marshal Tito, the head of the Yugoslavian government. Tito had founded a system of government based on communist teaching. At first he had been closely allied to the leaders of the Soviet Union. As he developed the government of his own country, he found it necessary to modify the standard Marxist doctrines. Mother discovered, upon her arrival, the difference between Soviet government policy and Yugoslavian policy. She was informed that the state did not run industry. Industry was operated by councils of workers. The workers quickly saw that good management was necessary, and that all must produce at their best level. It was obvious to Mother that the Yugoslavs were experimenting in an effort to find government theories that would permit limited individual freedom within a socialist framework. Mother's impression, as she went around Yugoslavia, was that decentralization of governmental power had been encouraged. She thought that this was rather remarkable in a dictatorship, where the leader or leaders usually want more instead of less power.

Tito had broken with the Soviet Union over his liberalized policies, but nowhere did Mother find any Yugoslavian who was worried about the danger of war. The workers were all intent upon giving their utmost to the jobs at hand. In one factory, they were making electrical transformers and other machinery needed for the development of power plants. Here she talked to one of the plant leaders. He said, "Our experts are new at this kind of thing, and they have made some mistakes, but last year we ran at a profit." "A profit?" Mother asked, mystified. "Oh yes, that is one of the incentives for high production. After taxes have been deducted, the workers' council divides the profits, one half going to pay interest and amortization on borrowed money or to improve the plant. The other half of the profits is divided among all the workers." Mother asked, "Do you think that arrangement has increased production?" The head of the workers' council smiled. "Of course it has," he said.

On the farms, Yugoslavia had at first followed the Soviet pattern of collective farming. This had not worked with the farmers, and the farming industry had changed over to permit small private farms and to encourage cooperative farming. Great progress had been made in public health and in education.

Marshal Tito, the head of Yugoslavia, discusses the Yugoslav system of government with Mother.   FRANKLIN D. ROOSEVELT LIBRARY

She went to Brioni, the lovely wooded island where the president's summer residence was located. His yacht was waiting near the shore. In this peaceful atmosphere, Mother arrived promptly at 10:00 in the morning at the president's villa. She was most impressed with her first sight of Marshal Tito because he seemed so youthful to her. His great charm and strong personality and sense of humor made an indelible mark. After their meeting at the villa, the marshal took her down to the dock. They got into a speedboat to go to a small island that he used as a retreat when he wished to be alone. The marshal himself piloted the speedboat and, with Mother beside him, he seemed to get a great deal of fun out of the experience.

One of the questions Mother asked of the president was, "Do you believe the people are contented under your socialist form of government?" Tito's answer came in the form of another question, "If you owned property and the government nationalized it, would you be contented?" Mother answered that she would not be happy about it at all. "Then I will say that I don't think everybody in Yugoslavia is content. But I believe the people realize that we are doing the things that will be best for our country in the long run." Mother wondered aloud whether he considered that his country was practicing communism.

His answer was, "Communism exists nowhere, least of all in the Soviet Union. Communism is an ideal that can be achieved only when people cease to be selfish and greedy, and when everyone receives according to his needs from communal production. But that is a long way off." He added, "I suppose that I might call myself a social democrat." He did not want what he was doing in Yugoslavia to be called communism, and he also objected to the use of the term "Titoism." He felt that every country should develop according to its own needs and that he did not want Yugoslavia to be held up as an example for others since Yugoslavia's system might not meet the needs of any other country. He insisted, "I am not a dictator. We have a group—all of us were partisans during the war—that works closely together and prepares for each step to be taken."

Mother came away from her meeting feeling that Tito had conceived of the present government as a step forward in the education of his people. Although she considered Marshal Tito a powerful and honest leader, I think that one of her lasting beliefs was that she would never want to live in Yugoslavia, nor would anyone else who valued personal freedom.

Mother had been agitating for a long while to have the opportunity of visiting the Soviet Union. This had not been possible while Stalin was alive, but by 1957, when Nikita

Mother's trip to Yugoslavia had its relaxing moments. *Left to right:* Her doctor and friend, David Gurewitsch, Marshal Tito, and Mother enjoy a day on Tito's yacht, off the island of Brioni.   FRANKLIN D. ROOSEVELT LIBRARY

Khrushchev had come to power, her visa was finally approved for her long-hoped-for visit. There is no question that this was one of the most important, most interesting, and most informative trips of her entire life. She spent almost a month within that country. She was not afraid of communist power or philosophy. She was not afraid of awesome missiles or hydrogen bombs. What she feared most was that we, in America, would not understand the nature of the Russian revolution that was going on and, in truth, is still going on today, and what it meant for the world. If we failed in this understanding, we would fail to protect world democracy and personal freedoms, no matter what missiles, earth satellites, or atomic warships we produced.

One of the inescapable impressions that Mother came away with from this trip was the enormous influence on the Russian people of Dr. Ivan Petrovich Pavlov, a physiologist and experimental psychologist. Mother knew that before his death Dr. Pavlov had conducted many experiments and made extensive studies of conditioned reflexes and that the Soviet government had built a special laboratory for him. It was while visiting Leningrad that she saw some of the results of his work, as she did in other parts of the country. She was convinced that he would become famous in history as the father of a system that seemed to be turning the masses of the Russian people into "completely disciplined and amenable people."

She visited an institute of medicine where thirty-two children taken at birth from lying-in hospitals, whose parents had died or abandoned them, were being trained. The purpose of the training was to see whether they could develop in an institution and be as advanced, healthy, and happy as in an ordinary home. In the nursery, a young woman in a white uniform and hat demonstrated the kind of training given the babies. It was here that Pavlovian theories were being put into practice. A six-month-old baby was brought to the nurse for his daily conditioning. The routine was simple. First the nurse held two rings out to the baby to persuade him to pull on them as the first step in his exercises. Mother noticed that the baby already knew what was coming and what he was supposed to do. He grasped the rings as soon as he saw the nurse. Then, after holding tightly to the rings throughout the exercise, he dropped them without being given any signal and shifted to the next exercise. This involved using his legs, and he went through the routine without any direction from the nurse. Then he lay rigid, waiting to be picked up by his heels and exercised while standing on his head. After that, the nurse picked him up and hugged and kissed him and spent some time playing with him, as any mother might do with a small baby. This attitude of affection and loving care was customary with children of different ages in the institutions that Mother visited.

The next group that Mother saw consisted of children about a year and a half old, who went through a more complicated routine. They came in like a drill team, took off their shoes, put them neatly in a row, and pulled out a bench from the wall. One after the other they crawled along the bench, then walked on it, then crawled under it. Then they climbed up on exercise bars. They knew exactly what to do and when to do it, like clockwork, and when they had finished the routine, each one walked over and sat on the lap of a nurse. The nurses lowered them down backward to the floor and pulled them up again in another exercise.Then the children put on their shoes, put the bench back in place, and went out.

Mother asked herself what this kind of training and behavior, which went on year after year, would mean in ordinary life outside the nursery or schoolroom. And as she watched the children, she knew that she had already seen some of the answers concerning the conduct of the Russian people. The Russian people she felt, were now raised according to the experiments of Dr. Pavlov and the conclusions that he had drawn about the conditioning of behavior. For this reason, the government was able to depend on the mass of the people to react in certain ways to certain stimuli. The Russian people were disciplined and well-trained, though not necessarily happy. Mother felt that Americans and the rest of the free world must not forget or ignore the distorted conditioning of the Russian people and also of the people in the developing countries whom the Communists sought to turn against the United States.

At the end of her trip, Mother visited Yalta where Father had held his last meeting of the Big Three. At Yalta, she met with

Nikita Khrushchev and she interviewed him at some length. While her interview was interesting and represented the thinking of Mr. Khrushchev, it would not necessarily represent the thinking of the current leaders of that country today. But I do think that Mother's conclusions from her visit to the Soviet Union are still valid: "It is not enough to say that we do not like the communist idea. We have to prove that our own idea is better and can accomplish more. We *can* accomplish more. . . . If we are to lead the free world, we must become a mature people—or we may one day wake up to find that fear and laziness have reduced us from a strong, vital nation to a people unable to lead other nations in the only way to win the struggle against communism, the way of the mind and the heart."

To Mother it was important that we have the courage to face ourselves in this crisis. We must regain a vision of ourselves as leaders of the world and join in an effort to use all knowledge for the good of all human beings. When we did that, we would have nothing to fear.

❧ 20 ☙

Back in the U.S.S.R.,
and Other Visits

In 1958, Mother had her second opportunity to visit the Soviet Union. She had been much troubled after her first visit. The more she had thought of that trip, the more troubled she had become. She felt that we, in America, were facing the greatest challenge to our way of life without any clear understanding about the facts. So, in 1958, she decided that she would like to return to the Soviet Union to confirm and expand on her earlier observations.

On this trip she had the opportunity of observing how older children were trained and educated. She told about the average child's existence and what it was like. She noted that it was far from easy. School started at 8:45 A.M. and went on until 1:45 P.M. If the children had anyone at home, they would then go home for a hot meal. Those with both parents absent were provided with their hot meal at school. After the meal, for the next two hours, they had exercises and supervised games. In addition, each day they were drilled in Marxism. Every child learned his Marxism backward and forward. There were two more hours of completely supervised outdoor games. The Russian child is never alone, and when the school day ends, he is assigned far more homework than an American child. By the time he leaves school, he takes not only his skills but, also, his political ideas with him wherever he might go.

At the age of fourteen, the majority of the students who have not been judged as capable of higher education are sent to technicons, a type of technical school. Here they stay for three years, until they are seventeen. At the age of seventeen, those that have graduated from the technicons are ready to take a job. Suddenly, they are thrown on their own and, except for the hours that they work, they are free. This limited freedom has caused monumental problems in the Soviet Union. These youngsters often create problems with their off-hour drinking and carousing.

As in any country, she observed, there is a large percentage of the youngsters who cannot be educated beyond a certain point. But in Russia there is a constant search for talent, for the exceptionally bright, for the artistically endowed, and for the scientifically minded. These young people are provided with every opportunity to improve their talents, to increase their learning, and to acquire as much education as they can absorb. Mother felt that the Soviet Union is the only country which pays the highest salaries and gives the highest honors to its artists and intellectuals, next to its politicians and scientists. She noted that in some basic ways the restrictions of life in Russia were the same, whether one was at the top or at the bottom of the scale. One rule seemed to hold true: There was practically no privacy in Russia. The number of rooms one was allotted depended upon the number of people who were to live in the dwelling. If there were four people, there were only two rooms. On the other hand, whether people were allotted two rooms or six rooms, the monthly rent was only 1 percent of their income.

She looked into the question of what happened to the children who were emotionally disturbed. She found that when these children were spotted by their teachers as having any deviation in behavior, they were reported immediately. Every school teacher was trained to watch for signs of physical, mental, or emotional disturbance. Where such disturbances seemed to be a result of home conditions, the social services worked to improve those conditions. Where more drastic efforts were needed, the child was sent to a sanitarium for preventive therapy. The health minister told Mother that inadequate housing in the big cities, bad relations between parents, and heavy drinking were the main reasons for these problems. Mother concluded that on the whole the Russians had fewer emotionally disturbed children and less of a problem with juvenile delinquency, particularly in the early years, than did Americans.

When Mother returned from the Soviet Union, late in the fall of 1958, she tried to compare her impressions against those of her first visit. The things that stood out most sharply were the changes that had taken place. On her first trip, there had been only trucks on the road. On the second, there were a number of small cars and a fair number of bigger cars, all of them of Russian make. On her first visit, new buildings were going up everywhere. On the second, a number of new apartments had been built in the city. On the first visit, people had appeared very drab. On the second, they were much better dressed, and they appeared at the end of the day's work to be happier and less anxious than they had been. This lessening of fear seemed to be a result of the greater time lapse since the repressive years under Stalin. In general, however, her second trip intensified her basic impressions from the first one.

Mother took two other trips in 1958 and 1959. In 1958, I accompanied her when she went to Morocco. What she found in Morocco was typical of the grave problems faced by the colonial countries that had emerged as free nations after World War II. When the French withdrew from Morocco, taking their nationals away, the towns and villages found themselves stripped of teachers and doctors. In practically every village, there was not a single person trained to give medical assistance, and the Moroccan government was not yet prepared to replace doctors, teachers, and service employees with their own people. The United States, through church organizations, had sent a considerable amount of food to alleviate the greatest need, but the conditions were still bad. People might be able to win their independence and freedom but they still were not prepared to set up a stable and functioning independent government. They were totally unprepared for self-government. This was true all over the African continent where so many new nations had come into being with the end of colonialism. Mother felt that colonialism was gone forever, but she felt strongly that some intermediate transition system was essential, if chaos were not to follow. The recent Afro-Asian resolution that had been passed in the UN best revealed the difficulty of the position by these words: "Inadequacy of political, economic, social or cultural preparedness" shall not serve as a pretext for denying independence. Mother felt that we could not ignore the fact that such a pretext had often been used in denying the right of self-determination. But it was evident that without some basic qualifications, self-determination would lead to self-destruction.

Her observations made back in 1958 have certainly come to pass in many of the new nations of Africa that emerged from the colonial era.

In 1959, she visited Iran and here she found a country existing in abject poverty. While Iran is not an Arabic nation, many of its problems are similar to those of the Arab nations of the Middle East. In Iran, the natural resources of the country had disappeared. Mind you, this was before the discovery of vast quantities of oil in Iran as well as in the Arab nations. The people on the whole lived in the greatest poverty, as well as in terrible health conditions. Iran had once had mighty forests. It had

One of the countries that Mother admired greatly was the new nation
of Israel, which she visited in 1959.   FRANKLIN D. ROOSEVELT LIBRARY

once been covered with fertile soil and ample lakes and rivers.
Now the land was a desert. The soil had been eroded and the
forests had disappeared. The people lived as nomadic tribes,
unwilling to settle down into village life. Preponderantly, they
were an illiterate population and education was not compul-
sory.

The conditions that she found to be true in Iran to a large
extent held true, as well, in all of the Arab nations of the Middle
East. When she went from Iran to Israel, she found an entirely
different atmosphere in Israel than in any of the Arab nations or

Iran. She felt that the greatest difference could be attributed to the young people, who were responsible for the electricity in the air. These young people were excited by the dream of building a country. They worked at it with gusto, and with all their strength, with exhilaration and a kind of exaltation, that could not fail to impress the visitor. The conditions were difficult, the labor long and hard, but they worked in an atmosphere of faith and hope and conviction. These were the qualities that were absent in the other countries. People cannot live without hope. She remarked at the time that even if hope was not engendered by their own convictions and desires, it could easily have been fired from without.

She had her own feelings as to how best to fire the imaginations and hearts of all of the people in the emerging nations of Africa and the hordes of very poor people living, with little hope, in the Middle Eastern Arab nations and Iran. She felt strongly that our country had a role to play in changing the outlook of these people and in giving them the opportunity to build viable and successful lives in their countries. She felt that we were failing in our efforts to help these young nations and those in transition to become established along democratic lines. The Russians, she thought, were doing a much better job. They were training their young people to go out into the world, to carry their services and skills to backward and developing nations; to replace the missing doctors, scientists, and technicians; and above all, to fill the vacant civil service jobs. The Russians were also briefing their young people in the customs, habits, traditions, and trends of thought of people in the developing nations so that they could understand and deal with these people. And wherever they went, of course, they brought their Marxist training, thinking, and system. If we Americans could practice what we preached, putting democracy to work and showing the world that our way of life has the most to offer the men and women and children of all countries, we could regain our lost leadership.

[*141*]

❧ 21 ☙

Tomorrow's Leaders

For many years, in fact right up to the time of her death, Mother had a deep-seated admiration and enthusiasm for the growth of the nation of Israel. She dedicated an enormous amount of personal energy to espousing that nation's efforts to transform its little slice of desert land into a vast new oasis of bustling productivity, not only from the land itself but from the industries being created. It is true that our government backed this new nation with massive aid, both economic and military. Also, the American Jewish community contributed mightily by raising large amounts of money through the purchase of Israel bonds, to insure success for the new democratic country.

Mother often wondered why Israel could so rapidly develop into the twentieth century when, all around her, other nations were struggling to bring their people out of poverty and ignorance and into the modern world. I know Mother must have realized that the population of Israel was made up of men, women, and children who had immigrated to this new land from all over the world. For the most part they were educated people, imbued with an intense desire to find individual freedom. These emigrés brought with them scientists, doctors, artists, and government technicians. This was a country well able to solve its own internal governing problems.

Israel's neighbors had no such capabilities. One reason for the hatred on the part of the Arab nations for the new nation of Israel was that the Arabs felt that some of their land had been taken from them and arbitrarily given to the Jews to create a competitive country within their midst. As a result, an endless struggle continued with the Arabs determined to run the Israelis off the small strip of land and the Israelis equally determined not to give one inch of their soil to the Arabs.

Mother realized all of these problems and she had her own program that she would have liked to have our country follow in bringing about a peaceful solution. Her thoughts followed along the lines of what she had seen the Russians accomplishing in training their young people for important posts in the emerging countries. The Russians were compelling their young people, but here, at home, we must do the same thing on a voluntary basis. It was her belief that we could show our youngsters the importance of acquiring the kind of training that would make them useful and honorable representatives of their country, wherever they might go abroad. Her theory was that the new frontier today "is something more than the new revolution in textiles and methods and speed and goods. It is the frontier of men's minds. But we cannot cast an enduring light on other men's minds unless the light in our own minds burns with a hard, unquenchable flame."

Mother believed that one form of communication we had failed in was the teaching of languages. During World War II, the government found a simplified and effective method of teaching such difficult languages as Japanese and Chinese to American GI's. In a matter of weeks, they had mastered more of the language than formerly they would have acquired in the same number of years. It seemed to her obvious that we must increase and improve the teaching of languages in the schools, otherwise our young people would find themselves crippled and handicapped in dealing with people of foreign races and different cultures.

Mother felt that our government should initiate an educational program starting with the earliest grades and going up through high school and college. This program would teach every student at least two foreign languages to the point where everyone could speak and write fluently in those languages. She advocated that all young people in our country should be imbued with the advantages of serving at home or abroad. It was her belief that the Peace Corps, which had been started under President John F. Kennedy, should be greatly enlarged to provide well-paid careers in emerging nations. These young people would assist in training service personnel from those countries to run their own government. They would assist in the building of sound agricultural and industrial economies and in modernizing the transport and communication systems. They would be paid by our government and would remain in the service as long as the emerging nations had a need for them.

In our own country, Mother advocated the revival of the Civilian Conservation Corps, which had been initiated way back in the New Deal era. Her vision of this corps was that young people who chose not to go on to a university could enlist in this branch of government employment. They would work on forestry, soil conservation, and the secondary road systems of the United States, and in clerical jobs at the governmental levels—city, county, state, and federal. The very essence of her belief in the future was that "every human being has a need to feel needed, to feel essential, to feel important."

Mother had strong feelings about the draft for the military. It was her opinion that a volunteer permanent organization should be maintained. In addition, she liked the Swiss method where every young person, male and female, went through several months of military training. After completing that training, they remained in the active reserve, subject to call in emergencies right up until their mid-forties. Under this plan, everybody gave two weeks out of every year to intensive training and preparedness. She felt that this was an equitable system and a good way for us to be able to defend ourselves in the event of outside attack.

My mother had an American dream. It was not a static dream but one that had the capability of change with changing times. She foresaw that automation and competition from without would change our industrial employment in this country. She felt that we could no longer sit by and let people starve and die if there were no jobs. If we were going to cope successfully, we would have to make the new techniques a blessing to society and not a disaster. We could not blunder along hoping that things "will come out all right." Government, industry, labor—all must use their best talent and brains, and accept their full responsibility for the situation. Masses of people now working at machines, without any opportunity for self-improvement or bettering their conditions, would be afforded new opportunities. But unless we could give them a background of education, they would not know how to make use of opportunity for advancement.

This was the belief of Mother way back before she died, over twenty years ago. She foresaw the new industrial revolution that we were pioneering. She felt that the eyes of the world were on us and that, if we did badly, we would be criticized and our way of life downgraded. If we did well, we could become a beacon light for the future of the world. What she felt then is even more true for us today. Her American dream was merely a new concept of the old one that had been promulgated by our Founding Fathers. Her advice for all young people was: "Do not stop thinking of life as an adventure. You have no security unless you can live bravely, excitingly, imaginatively; unless you can choose a challenge instead of a competence."

🎔 22 🎔

"Her Candle Has Lit the World"

During the last years of my mother's life, she devoted a great deal of time to promoting the work of the United Nations. She was concerned that many of the activities of the organization were overlooked and unappreciated by a vast majority of people.

Mother felt strongly that the United Nations needed to be restructured to make it more effective. She advocated that all arms, both nuclear and conventional, used in the waging of war, should be stockpiled and placed under the control of the United Nations. She felt that the United Nations should have a standing, multinational, military force prepared to step in and prevent any aggression by any nation against another, anywhere in the world. She felt that the United Nations should be able to enforce peaceful arbitration of any dispute arising between nations. She advocated a world code of law and justice. In short, she believed that the United Nations should be a supragovernment. It was her belief that all nations should adhere to the authority of the United Nations in insuring peaceful coexistence for all nations on this planet.

With John F. Kennedy, hours after he announced his candidacy for
the Democratic presidential nomination   UNITED PRESS INTERNA-
TIONAL

Mother had maintained her active participation in the Democratic political party over many years. In 1960, she took part in
her last big Democratic convention. She was firmly of the belief
that the best equipped man to be president of the United States
was Adlai Stevenson. She had consistently backed him in his
campaigns in 1952 and 1956. In 1960, she went to the Democratic convention in Los Angeles determined to fight for the
renomination of Adlai Stevenson.

Mother had three sons who were delegates to that convention: James, from California; myself, from Colorado; and

Addressing the 1960 Democratic National Convention on behalf of
the candidate Adlai Stevenson   UNITED PRESS INTERNATIONAL

[*148*]

Franklin, Jr., from New York. We were all pledged as delegates in support of John F. Kennedy. Mother came into the convention to second the nomination of her candidate, Adlai Stevenson. Later she commented: "Looking back on that turbulent—but prearranged—convention, I am heartened by the memory of the warm, spontaneous, outburst of genuine feeling and tribute and love that greeted Stevenson when he entered the hall to take his seat. Even though the delegates had been committed in advance, there was no stifling this tribute to a great statesman and a magnificent citizen."

I can recount the moment that Mother entered the convention hall. The convention itself went wild with the greatest and most spontaneous tribute to Mother that I think she ever received anywhere. The truth of the matter is, Mother almost swung those committed delegates away from the other candidates, John F. Kennedy and Lyndon Johnson. She almost carried the day for the renomination of Stevenson. Political rules being what they are, Kennedy was finally able to carry the day, and with Lyndon Johnson as his vice-presidential nominee, the Democrats went on to defeat the Republicans by a very close margin in the November election.

During the campaign, Mother was not sure of her feelings about young Jack Kennedy. Finally, he came to see her at Hyde Park, and she made up her mind that she could support him. So, once again, she took to the campaign trail in support of the Democratic nominee for the presidency, believing in her heart that he was a better candidate for the presidency than the Republican nominee, Richard Nixon. This was the last great political campaign of Mother's life. She had been actively participating in the political process for more than forty years.

The years 1961 and 1962 found Mother suffering more and more from various physical ailments. She had had as her physician and friend for many years, Dr. David Gurewitsch. He had looked after her many long-standing ailments so well that she was able to carry on her most strenuous schedule of travels and meetings.

One or two of the ailments that she had suffered from over the years had been the pain that she endured in her feet when called upon to stand for long periods of time. The other recurring ailment was a painful arthritic condition in her neck, shoulders, and upper spine. Because of his ministrations, she was able to endure the repeated strain that was placed on her. But, in 1961, in her seventy-seventh year, she began to suffer from an undetermined internal disorder. David Gurewitsch called in outside diagnosticians, and she underwent numerous tests. All kinds of antibiotics were prescribed, but by the spring of 1962, she had become much weaker.

Mother hated the idea of not being able to keep up with her engagements and obligations, but by June of 1962, she called me to find out if I could substitute for her in meeting some of her speaking obligations for the Bonds for Israel drive. This I agreed to do, but she still insisted on trying to keep up with the rest of her schedule. By September, David was so concerned about her condition that he forced her to go to the hospital. There her condition was diagnosed as being aplastic anemia. This was a condition of an imbalance between the white and red corpuscles of the blood.

By her seventy-eighth birthday, on October 11, 1962, her condition had deteriorated still further. She had been taken to the hospital in September, and this time the diagnosis was that she had a flare-up of tuberculosis. She had evidently had, in her younger years, a slight attack, but now the doctors confirmed that it had returned. Mother did not want to die in the hospital. She sensed that her death was imminent, and so she asked to be taken from the hospital back to her little house in New York City. There, a constant vigil was set up by her five children and their spouses. This was an excruciating time for all of us. We watched our mother as she drifted in and out of consciousness, during those last days. We became resigned to the fact that she would never again be able to carry on her efforts on behalf of all people everywhere.

On November 7, she finally passed away. The funeral took place at Hyde Park, where she was interred next to Father in the rose garden of our old family home. She was finally reunited with her husband, and partner, of many, many years. The president, vice president, and two former presidents, and all the major political leaders of our country came to pay their respects at her grave. They were joined by the leaders of many other countries and all their ambassadors.

On this momentous day, we—Mother's five children and our spouses—all gathered at the grave site where Father had been buried.

Members of the family stood to the right of her grave, and the dignitaries all gathered on the left, facing the grave site. We followed the same procedure at my mother's funeral that had been used at Father's burial. As I stood there during the service, I glanced to the left and could see former President Truman, former President Eisenhower, Vice President Johnson, and President Kennedy, all standing with heads bared in tribute to a woman who had had an enormous influence on their lives and times. Ranged behind these dignitaries were representatives of many of the nations on earth. Behind the members of the immediate family, to the right, stood a host of close personal friends and relatives, whose entire lives had been intertwined with the activities of Eleanor Roosevelt for more than fifty years. The huge number of floral tributes sent by heads of foreign governments and thousands of individuals who wanted to pay a last tribute to their former first lady were massed and banked on three sides of the grave.

The burial ceremony, simple but impressive, and this last tribute to Mother, would remain forever engraved in the memory of all of us who were there on that day. There were two memorial services following the burial at Hyde Park. One was held in New York at the Cathedral of St. John the Divine, the other at the National Cathedral in Washington, D.C. All the members of the family attended both. The one in New York enabled many of those who had worked with Mother in the United Nations, or been associated with her down through the years, to attend and listen to a remarkable eulogy by Adlai Stevenson, who said, "Her candle has lit the world." The ceremony at the National Cathedral in Washington, D.C., was attended by most members of the Senate, the House of Representatives, members of the Cabinet, members of the Supreme Court, and large numbers of government workers. Dean Rusk, our secretary of state in the Kennedy Administration, spoke with great simplicity and gave a beautiful tribute to Mother's memory. It was hard to realize that she was gone, and that we could no longer count on her as a family for her support and loving advice, as we had for so many, many years.

Epilogue

I have recorded many of the vicissitudes that were visited upon my mother, Anna Eleanor Roosevelt, during her lifetime. I have recorded how she overcame all of these challenges and rose above them to eventually become, without any doubt, the outstanding woman of the world in the twentieth century. She accomplished this without ever having been elected to high office, without ever enlisting any organized group or religion on her behalf, and using solely the force of her own personality and philosophy, to exert her worldwide influence.

It is perfectly true, that during the course of her career, my mother attracted many people who were in violent disagreement with her efforts. She had many detractors who were opposed to her views. Many writers scorned her activities and felt that she was an unbearable nuisance. On the other hand, the flood of mail which inundated her throughout her career attested to her acceptance by many as a truly great leader. These letters came from the great and the small in all walks of life, and from every section of the world. They buoyed her and strengthened her determination to carry on until the very end of her life.

The basic principles by which she lived were:

"Do unto others as you would have them do unto you."

"I am my brother's keeper."

"We are all the children of God, and we must all do his bidding."

I believe that if we follow her example and her beliefs, we can solve the frightening problems that beset all of us today, and we can move toward the goal of achieving peace and well-being for all of the people of the world.

FURTHER READING

Mother wrote voluminously, and aside from her daily column, "My Day," and her magazine articles, she wrote several autobiographies. In this book, I quote from some of my mother's work. For the reader who would be interested in reading Mother's books, here is a partial list.

The Autobiography of Eleanor Roosevelt. New York: Harper & Row, 1961.
On My Own. New York: Harper & Row, 1958.
This I Remember. Westport, Connecticut: Greenwood, 1975.
This Is My Story. New York: Harper & Brothers, 1937.
Tomorrow Is Now. New York: Harper & Row, 1963.
You Learn by Living. New York: Harper & Row, 1960.

Index

Page numbers in *italics* refer to captions.

ABOUT THE AUTHOR

ELLIOTT ROOSEVELT had a distinguished career as a briga-
dier general during World War II, earning the Legion of
Merit, two Distinguished Flying Crosses, and ten Air
Medals. He was named Commander of the Order of the
British Empire, awarded the French Croix de Guerre with
two palms, and admitted to the Legion d'Honneur.

He served in the 1960s as mayor of Miami Beach.
Before that, he was active in the radio and television
industries, and in the 1930s was involved in aviation.
Throughout his life, Mr. Roosevelt has had an abiding interest in agriculture.

He has written many best-selling reminiscences about
his family and has edited the personal letters of his father,
President Franklin Delano Roosevelt.

Mr. Roosevelt and his wife live in Palm Desert, California.

92
ROOSE
VELT
Roosevelt, Elliott
Eleanor Roosevelt,
with love

17389

7·93

DATE